WHY

is Jesus?

...And Why Should I Care?

WHY
is Jesus?

...And Why
Should I Care?

Open your mind and your heart for incredible events and an adventure.
You may be surprised what you discover and experience.

For Ages 16 to 116

J.E. Daniels

Why Is Jesus?
...And Why Should I Care?

© 01/2024 J.E. Daniels

The Authorized (King James) Version of the Bible ('the KJV'), the rights in which are vested in the Crown of the United Kingdom, is reproduced here by permission of the Crown's patentee, Cambridge University Press.

Published by Carpenter's Son Publishing, Franklin, Tennessee

Edited by Ann Tatlock

Cover Design by Suzanne Lawing

Interior Design by J.E. Daniels

Printed in the United States of America

ISBN 978-1-956370-16-4

Note: Jewish people are called Jews, Hebrews, and Israelites.
For the entire story, see Exodus in the Old Testament and referenced books in the New Testament.
In places, italics, bold, capitals, and colors have been used for emphasis.
Unless otherwise noted, scripture references are from the **King James Version** (KJV) of the **Bible**.

Dedicated to All Those Who Recognize and Cherish Truth!

Who Is Jesus?

Jesus is the Son of God. He is amazing!
"In the beginning was the Word, and the Word was with God, and the
Word was God." (John 1:1)

Sometimes Jesus is called the "Word." Jesus was with God the Father
from the beginning of time in Heaven and helped God create everything.
God and Jesus have worked together to bring us an incredible universe,
life, Heaven, and afterlife. (Also see Hebrews 1:2)

However, to understand who Jesus is, we need to start by learning more
about God. Back to Jesus in a bit.

~A long, long time ago, Abraham learned that God was real, and he began
serving God. God promised Abraham that a great nation of people would
come from Abraham. They are the Jewish people, also called the Hebrews
and the Israelites.

God Freed His People from Slavery in Egypt

God Frees His People from Slavery to Sin

We need to begin with the following story so we can understand the whole plan.

This story is important and astonishing.

The Hebrews were slaves in Egypt for over four hundred years.
Slavery is horrible and should **never** happen to anyone. The people lived
in awful conditions and were severely mistreated.
Working hard, they had to make bricks from straw and build whatever
Pharaoh commanded.

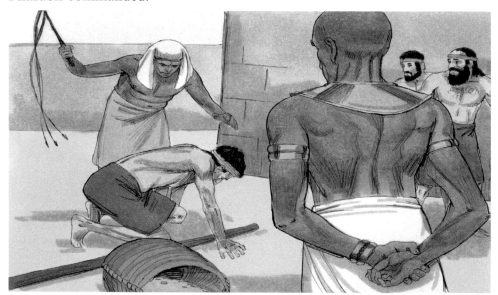

The slaves worked very hard every day and suffered much abuse.

5

The Hebrews prayed mightily for God to free them from slavery.

6

Moses was saved for this purpose. When Moses was born, there was a decree from Pharaoh that all Hebrew baby boys were to be killed. Moses's mother put baby Moses in a basket and sent him into the river. Moses's sister, Miriam, hid and watched to see what would happen to him. Pharaoh's daughter, who wanted a child but had none, found baby Moses. She took him out of the water and raised him as her own. Moses grew up as a Prince of Egypt and was used to seeing the Hebrews as slaves. (See Exodus 2:5)

When Moses was older, he learned the truth about his birth and rescue and that his people were the slaves! While Moses was visiting the Hebrew slaves, he witnessed one of them being beaten. Moses killed the cruel Egyptian who beat the slave. Because he had killed the Egyptian, Moses fled to the land of Midian to save his own life. He was gone many years.

Moses married Zipporah, the daughter of Jethro, and had a family. Jethro and Moses were good to each other. (See Exodus 2:11-16)

Later, answering the slaves' prayers for their freedom, the Lord appeared to Moses at the burning bush. God told Moses, "Put off thy shoes from off thy feet, for the place whereon thou standest is holy ground." (Exodus 3:5) God called Moses to deliver the slaves from bondage.

Moses could not believe God wanted him to be part of freeing the slaves. He thought the slaves would not believe that the Lord spoke to him. Moses was also concerned about his speaking abilities and argued that he was slow of speech. God advised Moses to take his brother, Aaron, with him to help him speak to the people.

The Lord allowed Moses to perform miracles so the people would believe he had been chosen for their aid. One miracle was Moses's rod (staff) becoming a serpent when he cast it on the ground. When Moses picked the serpent up by the tail, it became the rod again. (See Exodus 4:1-4 and 14-15)

The Lord also identified Himself to Moses as the God of Abraham, Isaac, and Jacob; I AM; God Almighty and Jehovah. (See Exodus 3:6,14 and 6:3)

God told Moses He would smite Egypt and bring His people out of that country with gold and silver. (See Exodus 3:21-22) Moses took his wife and his sons to Egypt, as he had been told. (See Exodus 4:20) Aaron also came.

God told Moses to go talk to Pharaoh. "And thou shalt say unto him, The Lord God of the Hebrews hath sent me unto thee, saying, Let my people go." (Exodus 7:16 [Also Exodus 5:1, 8:1, 8:20, 9:1, 9:13, 10:3-4])

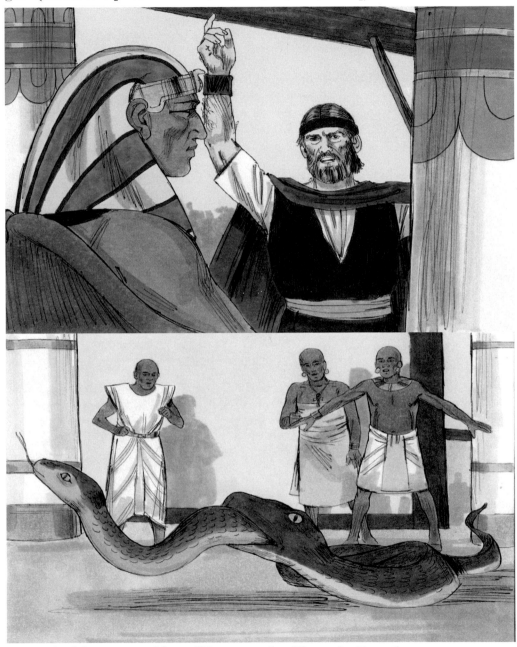

Moses had Aaron turn his staff into a snake. Then, the Egyptian sorcerers and magicians also turned their rods into snakes. *Aaron's snake promptly ate all the other snakes.* (See Exodus 7:9-12)

"And the Lord said unto Moses, Pharaoh's heart is hardened, he refuseth to let the people go." (Exodus 7:14)

The Lord told Moses to have Aaron put his rod into the river, and **the water was turned into blood.**

The fish died, and it stank. (See Exodus 7:17-21)

Some of the Egyptian magicians and sorcerers mimicked what Moses and Aaron did, and Pharaoh would still not let the slaves go. The people could not drink the river water, and the river remained blood for seven days. (See Exodus 7: 22-25)

Per God's instruction, Moses sent various plagues on Egypt.

Massive amounts of frogs swarmed all over Egypt. Frogs were everywhere. Pharaoh summoned Moses and Aaron and said, "Intreat the Lord, that he may take away the frogs from me, and from my people; and I will let the people go…" (Exodus 8:8) Then Moses prayed, and the frogs died.

They gathered the dead frogs into heaps "and the land stank." (Exodus 8:14)

Yet, Pharaoh did **not** let the slaves go as he promised!

11

Next, God had Moses and Aaron send lice throughout all the land of Egypt. The Egyptian magicians tried to replicate this plague, but they could not. The magicians told Pharaoh, "This is the finger of God." (Exodus 8:19 [See Exodus 8:16-19])

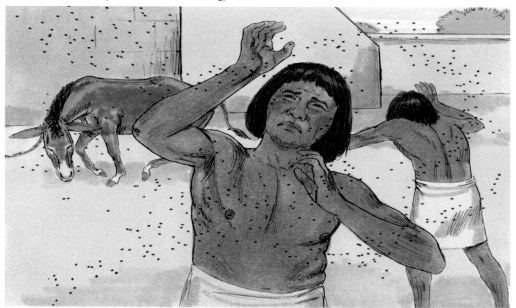

Again, Pharaoh's heart remained hardened, and he would not free the Hebrew slaves. As each plague ended, Pharaoh continued to break his promises to let the slaves go.

God had Moses say to Pharaoh, "Thus saith the Lord, Let my people go, that they may serve me. Else, if thou wilt not let my people go, behold, I will send **swarms of flies** upon thee, and upon thy servants, and upon thy people, and into thy houses: and the houses of the Egyptians shall be **full of swarms of flies,** and also the ground whereon they are." (Exodus 8:20-21)

True to form, Pharaoh stood firm in his stance and continued to change his mind about freeing the slaves. So, as promised, the flies came.

Pharaoh would not let the slaves go free. Thus numerous plagues and bad things continued.

Again, God warned Pharaoh of what would happen, but Pharaoh refused to listen or let the Hebrew people have their freedom. The next plague came. **All the Egyptian cattle, horses, donkeys, oxen, camels, and sheep died.**

Because God declared, "And there shall nothing die of all that is the children's of Israel." (Exodus 9:4) None of the slaves' animals died.

The Lord means what He says.

*All of the plagues attacked the Egyptians, but **none** of them attacked the Hebrew slaves or their animals.*

Even still, Pharaoh lied, saying he would let the people go. He instead kept them enslaved. (See Exodus 9:1-7)

There was also a plague of **boils and blisters** called blains. The Egyptian magicians could not stand before Moses because they had boils. Pharaoh still hardened his heart and would not let the slaves go. (See Exodus 9:8-11)

Under God's direction, Moses sent **hail/ice and fire** to soften Pharaoh's heart, but Pharaoh's heart remained hardened. (See Exodus 9:22-28)

Then a **horrible swarm of locusts** came that ate everything, even the trees. (See Exodus 10:4-15)

Pharaoh said to Moses, "Forgive, I pray thee, my sin…" Pharaoh wanted the locusts removed. So, the Lord sent a mighty east wind that took away all the locusts. However, Pharaoh would still **not** let the slaves go, **even though he promised he would.** (See Exodus10:12-19)

Next, Egypt experienced **three days of thick darkness** that could be felt. It was so dark that people could not see one another. Yet, the Hebrew slaves had light. (See Exodus 10:21-23)

Another plague was underway. In preparation for leaving Egypt, the slaves got jewels of silver and jewels of gold from their Egyptian neighbors. (See Exodus 11:2) Many of the Egyptian people wanted the slaves gone after the nine plagues they had endured. However, the worst plague was yet to come.

Ultimately, there was no stopping the last plague. Moses listened to the Lord and had the Hebrew slaves prepare for this plague. Moses told them to paint the two side front door posts and upper front door post, called a lintel, of each house with blood from an unblemished male lamb. They were to stay inside their houses and eat as directed. (See Exodus 12:5, 7-8)

"And thus shall ye eat, with your loins girded, with your shoes on your feet, and your staff in your hand; and ye shall eat in haste: it is the Lord's passover." (Exodus 12:11)

That night, *all* **the firstborn Egyptians and beasts died**, but *none* of the Hebrew people or their animals died. (See Exodus 11:5-7)

Understandably, all of the Egyptians were upset over the death of their firstborn, while none of the firstborn among the Hebrews died. The death of the Egyptians was the worst plague of all.

Saved by the Blood of the
Passover Lamb in Egypt

Saved by the Blood of the
Lamb, Jesus, Today

The angel of death skipped/**passed over** all Israelite homes because of the blood of an unblemished male lamb on each of their front door frames. Thus began "Passover," and it is celebrated each and every year to this day.

The unblemished lamb's blood on their front door posts saved all the firstborn Hebrew slaves and all their animals from dying. The blood of a lamb saved them. They were protected. The Egyptian firstborn deaths, including the death of Pharaoh's son, finally got Pharaoh to listen and to let the Israelite slaves/people go free.

God freed the Israelite people from the slavery that they endured for four hundred thirty (430) years!

The Israelite (Jewish/Hebrew) slaves being saved by the lamb's blood was a foreshadowing of what was to come. *Jesus* is called the "*Lamb of God*," and the shedding of *His innocent blood* allows *all of us* the opportunity to be saved. More on this very important part of Moses's story later.

We will learn more about Jesus as the unblemished Lamb of God who was sacrificed for *each of us*.

Happy Passover!

When the Israelite people were heading to the promised land, Pharaoh changed his mind about letting them go free. He sent his army of six hundred chosen chariots to recapture the slaves. (See Exodus 14:5-9)

The Hebrew people found themselves trapped between Pharaoh's racing army and a large body of water, the Red Sea. The people panicked! They did not want to be enslaved again.

Next, they did what **we all need to do** when we are in trouble:
"The children of Israel cried out unto the Lord."
(Exodus 14:10)

Through prayer and the Lord, they were freed from slavery, and it would only be prayer and the Lord that could save them now. They were in a really precarious situation.

Some of the people were so afraid that they just wanted to give up and go back with the Egyptians to be slaves again. They thought that it would be better to serve the Egyptians than to die.

"And Moses said unto the people, Fear ye not, stand still, and see the salvation of the Lord, which he will shew to you to day: for the Egyptians whom ye have seen to day, ye shall see them again no more for ever.

"The Lord shall fight for you, **and ye shall hold your peace.**" (Exodus 14:13-14)

God instructed Moses, "Lift thou up thy rod, and stretch out thine hand over the sea, and divide it: and the children of Israel shall go on dry ground through the midst of the sea." (Exodus 14:16)

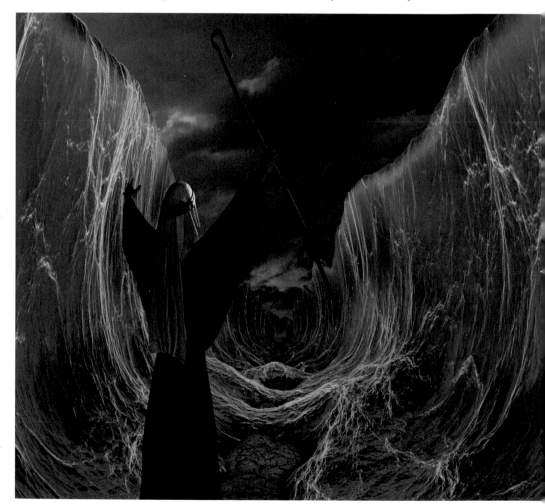

The Red Sea Parted
As everyone watched, the water rose up on either side, revealing dry land.

Dry land was created for the Israelites to escape.
It was miraculous!

The water was held back until all the Jewish people were able to cross on dry land.

After the freed slaves crossed the Red Sea on dry land, the water returned to where it had been just as Pharaoh's army was trying to cross, drowning them all. This miracle stopped Pharaoh's army from pursuing the Hebrew people ever again. (See Exodus 14:16-31)

Miraculous.

The freed slaves traveled to the mountain in the desert where God first spoke to Moses at the burning bush: Mt. Sinai.

They celebrated their new freedom and praised the Lord. Miriam, Moses's sister, led them in dance and song. She said, "Sing ye to the Lord, for He hath triumphed gloriously." (See Exodus 15:20-21)

Later, Moses went up to the mountaintop to talk to the Lord again.

The Hebrew people witnessed the various plagues sent upon the Egyptians, but not upon them. They experienced many miracles and gained their long-awaited freedom after being slaves for centuries!

Were they thankful? Were they good?

Very quickly, while Moses was up on the mountain seeking the Lord, the newly freed people started partying, doing things and acting in ways they should not. The freed slaves even demanded Aaron make them a golden calf to worship instead of praising and worshiping God.

They began melting gold for their calf idol, and their evil actions worsened. These people allowed the Egyptian ways to which they had been subjected to influence them instead of **staying true to the Lord.**

What an abomination!

On the mountaintop, the Lord wrote the Ten Commandments on two stone tablets and gave them to Moses.

When Moses came down the mountain and saw what the people were doing, he was furious.

They should not have been worshipping a golden calf, an idol, as the Egyptians did. They should have been thanking God for the miraculous gift of their **precious freedom.**

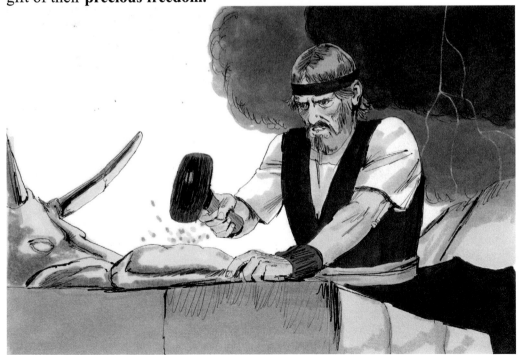

We all need to be careful of who and what we let influence us.

27

Think a moment on how you are blessed. How often are we too busy or forget to thank God for what He has helped us with or even solved? We all need to do better.

Once the pressure is off, we tend to forget God. We should not do that. We never want God to forget us, and He never will.

Aaron felt awful for being part of creating the golden calf, but he was **afraid to go against the crowd**.

Has that ever happened to you?

We all get scared at times.

Sometimes, it is hard to stand up for what is right or to help others, but God will give us strength and protection if we turn to Him and ask for help. It may not be easy, but ***it is always worth it!***

The Ten Commandments
Then and Now

Thou shalt have no other gods before me

Thou shalt not make unto thee any graven image

Thou shalt not take the name of the Lord thy God in vain

Remember the sabbath day, to keep it holy

Honor thy father and thy mother

Thou shalt not kill

Thou shalt not commit adultery

Thou shalt not steal

Thou shalt not bear false witness against thy neighbor

Thou shalt not covet

God gave Moses ten rules called the Ten Commandments for the freed Israelite people **and us** to live by and follow. (See Exodus 20:2-17)

1) *"Thou shalt have no other gods before me."* Often, people make things their god without even realizing it. Money or career, house or car, sports or another person, celebrities or fame. The list goes on …

2) *"Thou shalt not make unto thee any graven image."* We were meant to worship, love, and appreciate God the Father. Do not create any object into which to pour worship.

3) *"Thou shalt not take the name of the Lord thy God in vain."* This commandment is broken most often without people even realizing. It simply becomes a very bad habit. One of the meanings of "in vain" is *"for no purpose."* To be safe, only say God's name, whichever one you are using, when you are **talking to God or about God**. Never use any of His names as a slang word or something to just call out when you are upset, angry, frustrated, or even excited or happy.

The same is true of the name of Jesus Christ. If you are saying His name, only do so if and when you are talking **to Him or about Him**.

"We only have a few rules around here, but we really enforce them."

4) *"Remember the sabbath day to keep it holy."* We should not work on Sunday. Instead, we go to church, help others, and worship God. (There are references, however, about doing *necessary* things on Sunday in the Bible, like rescuing the ox. Some medical professionals, fire fighters, and others need to work on Sunday. Just be cautious about what is actually *necessary*. (See Luke 14:5, 13:15)

5) *"Honour thy father and thy mother."* Honor means "to respect." Hopefully, you have wonderful parents. If you do, thank God for them. Unfortunately, not everybody does. If you do not have at least one loving parent, grandparent, or guardian, please know that God does still love you very much. One day, you can be the mom or dad you wish you had had as a kid. God will help you do that.

6) *"Thou shalt not kill."* God should decide time of death.

7) *"Thou shalt not commit adultery."* A husband and wife should always remain faithful to each other.

8) *"Thou shalt not steal."* Self explanatory.

9) *"Thou shalt not bear false witness."* Do not lie.

10) *"Thou shalt not covet."* You should not be jealous of or want what other people have. You may like what you see and want one similar to theirs, but you should not want what actually belongs to them. Instead, you should be thankful for what God has given you.

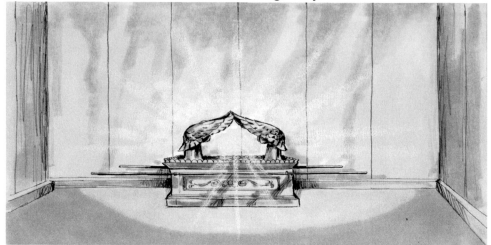

The Ark of the Covenant holds the Ten Commandments.

These Ten Commandments are the basic rules God wants us to follow— the bare minimum—and mostly common sense. Some countries' laws are based on the Ten Commandments.

Living by and following the Ten Commandments helps you to have a much better life. It also helps your entire family when you keep the commandments.

Our Father in Heaven and Jesus Christ want us to have the very best life, and very best afterlife, we possibly can—for ourselves and our for loved ones. Keeping *all* of the Ten Commandments helps us to achieve this goal.

One important point before we continue: Some people think money is evil. Money is *not* evil. The ***love*** of money is the problem. The Bible says, "For the *love* of money is the root of all evil." (1 Timothy 6:10, emphasis mine) Money is a necessity and can and should be used to help people and to do good.

We are now heading to some incredible parts of the overall plan!

Heavenly Love

Do You Know How Much God Loves You?

The Bible tells us, "For God so loved the world, that he gave his only begotten Son, that whosoever believeth in him should not perish, but have everlasting life." (John 3:16)

It sometimes takes a while for people to grasp the amount of *love* that God has for *us*. When you think about what *Jesus did for us* and what *God let* Him accomplish and endure, the amount of *love* that God has for you and me is staggering. It is breathtaking. It is overwhelming. It is almost incomprehensible! Just *always remember that you are loved very much by our Father in Heaven and Jesus Christ—more than you know or realize.*

Baby Jesus—
"For the law was given by Moses, but grace and truth came by Jesus Christ." (John 1:17)

Young Mary was visited by an angel and told that she was going to have a baby, the Son of God. "And the angel said unto her, Fear not, Mary: for thou hast found favour with God." (Luke 1:30)
Mary was a virgin. So, she was confused at first by what she was told. But Mary listened to the angel.

"And the angel answered and said unto her, The Holy Ghost shall come upon thee, and the power of the Highest shall overshadow thee: therefore also that holy thing which shall be born of thee shall be called the Son of God." (Luke 1:35 [Also see Matthew 1:18]) This miracle is how Jesus came to be.

Mary was already engaged to Joseph when the angel spoke to her. When Joseph found out Mary was expecting a child, he was not sure what to do. So, an angel visited Joseph to let him know that they should get married as planned.

"But while he thought on these things, behold the angel of the Lord appeared unto him in a dream, saying, Joseph, thou son of David, fear not to take unto thee Mary thy wife: for that which is conceived in her is of the Holy Ghost." (Matthew 1:20)

"And she shall bring forth a son, and thou shalt call his name *JESUS*: for *he shall save his people from their sins.*" (Matthew 1:21)

As good, law-abiding citizens, Mary and Joseph traveled from their home town of Nazareth all the way to Bethlehem in order to pay their taxes. Mary was near the end of her pregnancy, so she rode a donkey as Joseph led the way. When they finally reached Bethlehem, baby Jesus was ready to be born.

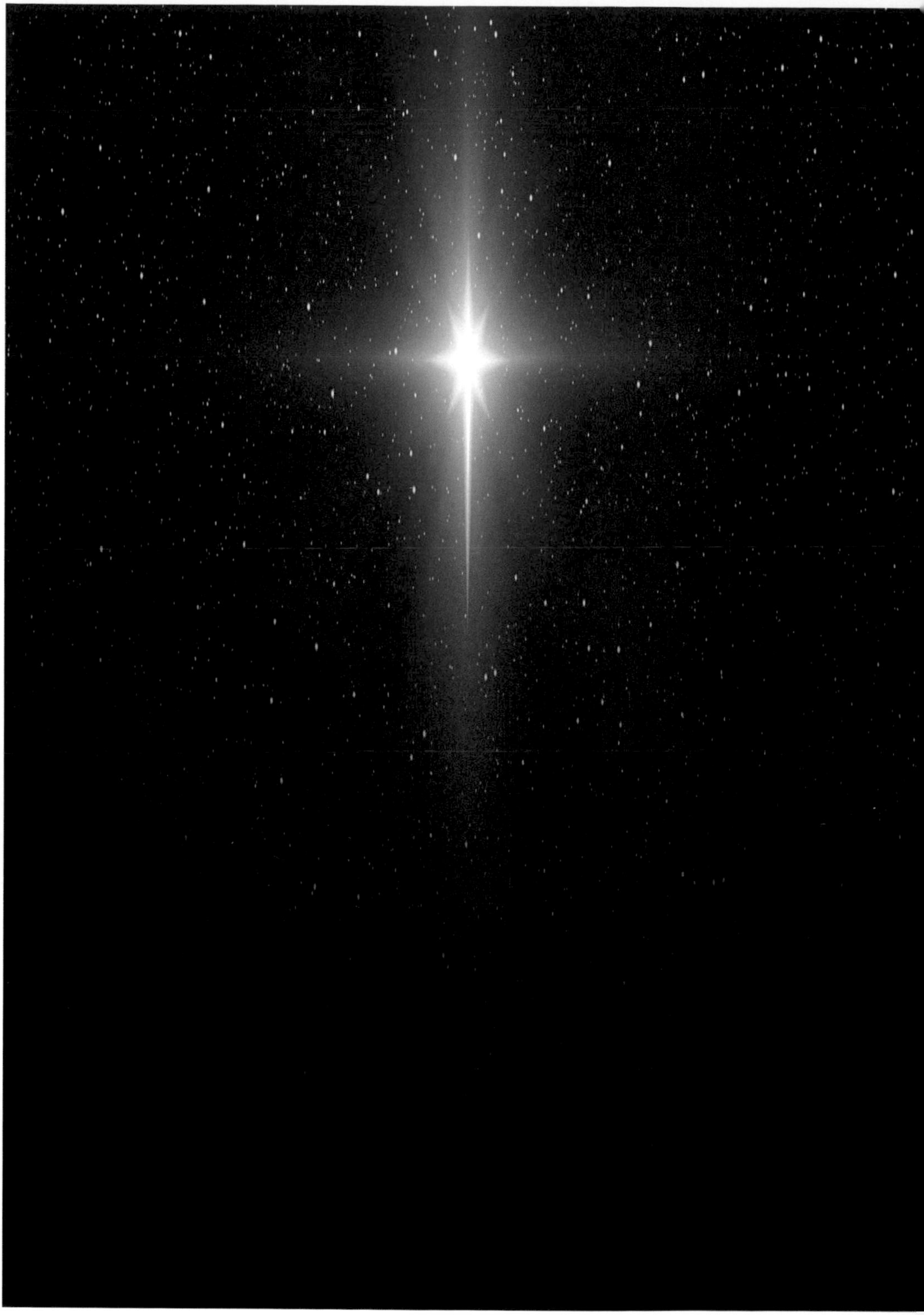

Jesus
Is
Born

Joseph tried to get a room at the inn in Bethlehem, which was like a hotel, but all the rooms were full. So, the innkeeper said they could stay in the stable with the animals. Joseph likely made Mary a bed out of straw, and, for sure, there was also a manger there. (See Luke 2:7, 12, 16)

So, baby Jesus was born in a stable with the cows and sheep and donkeys. He was wrapped in swaddling clothes and placed in the manger.

The Son of God arrived on earth *to save us all.*

Swaddling clothes are soft strips of cloth used to wrap newborn babies to keep them warm. They are also used to wrap baby lambs, and remember, Jesus is called the "Lamb of God." (John 1:29, 36)

The Star of Bethlehem guided people to Jesus.

There was a large, beautiful star over the stable. The shepherds watched.

"And there were in the same country shepherds abiding in the field, keeping watch over their flock by night.

"And, lo, the angel of the Lord came upon them, and the glory of the Lord shone round about them: and they were sore afraid.

"And the angel said unto them, Fear not: for, behold, I bring you good tidings of great joy, which shall be to all people.

"For unto you is born this day in the city of David [Bethlehem] a Saviour, which is Christ the Lord." (Luke 2:8-11)

"Ye shall find the babe wrapped in swaddling clothes, lying in a manger." (Luke 2:12)

"And suddenly there was with the angel a multitude of the heavenly host praising God, and saying, Glory to God in the highest, and on earth peace, good will toward men." (Luke 2:13-14)

The shepherds rushed to the stable to see *baby Jesus*. (See Luke 2:15-17)

Jesus accepted His earthly mission and was **born to help all of us.**

Later, three wise men came searching for *baby Jesus* to see and *worship the newborn King of the Jews*. They brought gifts with them to give to Jesus. (For the whole story, see Matthew 2:1-21)

The wise men inquired of King Herod. He was an evil and terrible king. When he heard a King was born, he wanted the new King gone. Herod told the wise men, "Go and search diligently for the young child; and when ye have found him, bring me word again, that I may come and worship him also." (Matthew 2:8) Herod was totally lying about why he wanted to know where Jesus was located.

"Lo, the star, which they saw in the east, went before them, till it came and stood over where the young child was." The wise men "rejoiced with exceeding great joy." (Matthew 2:9-10)

When the wise men saw Jesus, they "fell down, and worshipped him: and when they had opened their treasures, they presented unto him gifts; gold, and frankincense, and myrrh." (Matthew 2:11)

The wise men, "being warned of God in a dream that they should not return to Herod, they departed into their own country another way." (Matthew 2:12)

"Behold, the angel of the Lord appeareth to Joseph in a dream, saying, Arise, and take the young child and his mother, and flee into Egypt, and be thou there until I bring thee word: for Herod will seek the young child to destroy him." (Matthew 2:13)

So, Joseph took Mary and Jesus immediately to Egypt, as the angel instructed. They remained there to keep Jesus safe.

Herod was furious that the wise men did not return to tell him where to find Jesus "and sent forth, and slew [killed] all the children that were in Bethlehem, and in all the coasts thereof, from age two years old and under." (Matthew 2:16)

With the help of the angel, Joseph, Mary, and Jesus had already escaped before Herod enacted his horrible plan.

"But when Herod was dead, behold, an angel of the Lord appeareth in a dream to Joseph in Egypt, Saying, Arise, and take the young child and his mother, and go into the land of Israel: for they are dead which sought the young child's life." (Matthew 2:19-20)

So, after Herod's death, Joseph, Mary, and Jesus returned to live in Nazareth, their home.

When Jesus was twelve years old, the family planned to go to Bethlehem for a while. As they were leaving, Joseph and Mary could not find Jesus. (See Matthew 2:40)

Mary and Joseph looked everywhere for Jesus for three days.

"After three days they found him [Jesus] in the Temple, sitting in the midst of the doctors, both hearing them and asking them questions.

"And all that heard him were astonished at his understanding and answers. And when they [Mary and Joseph] saw him, they were amazed." (Luke 2:46-48)

When Joseph and Mary found Jesus with these learned men, they were also astounded at the questions Jesus asked and all that He understood.

Despite their amazement, Mary and Joseph were sad Jesus worried them when He could not be found. Mary said to Jesus, "Son, why hast thou thus dealt with us? behold, thy father and I have sought thee sorrowing. And he [Jesus] said to them [Mary and Joseph] *How is it that ye sought me* [meaning, looked for Him]? *wist ye not that I must be about my Father's business?*" (Luke 2:48-49, emphasis mine)

Jesus was referring to God, His (and our) Father in Heaven, and admitting that He had a *job to do and important things to accomplish!*

Jesus was sorry He scared Mary and Joseph, so he went home with them to Nazareth. "And Jesus increased in wisdom and stature, and in favour with God and man." (Luke 2:52)

Joseph was a carpenter and taught Jesus many skills.

Jesus was referred to as the carpenter's son. (See Matthew 13:55)

However, people also called Jesus a carpenter. "Is not this the carpenter, the son of Mary…" (Mark 6:3)

Jesus learned countless things from God and from those around Him as He grew both physically and spiritually.

Before we continue, there are some important things we need to know, consider, and understand.

The War in Heaven!

The War in Heaven

Many people are unaware of a crucial event called the War in Heaven, and are equally unaware of its daily impact on our lives.

The Bible clearly tells us about the War in Heaven. Long before Jesus was born on earth, there was a war in Heaven. Lucifer, who was the "son of the morning," rebelled against God. (See Isaiah 14:12-15) Lucifer wanted the other angels to follow and worship him instead of God.

Most of the angels wanted to be good and love and follow God. Lucifer tried desperately to get everyone to be bad but only got some of the angels on his side. Michael, the archangel (see Jude 1:9), and the good angels fought Lucifer and the bad angels. (See Revelation Chapter 12)

The Bible tells how Lucifer (also now called Satan or the devil) and the other bad angels were sent down to Earth. God said they could no longer be in Heaven and cast them out. (See Revelation 12:7-14, 17)

Satan and his evil spirit followers are on Earth **trying to get people to choose evil over good.** They want everyone to be bad and miserable the way they are all the time. However, *God gave us a very special gift—*

We get to choose for ourselves: be good or be bad.
That is the only way we can truly grow and learn.

We make many choices every day. As God's children, we are bound for Heaven. It is very important that we make good choices and do good things. Satan and his evil followers always try to get people to choose evil and deny God's gift of salvation. They are jealous that they will never get to go back to Heaven—and they do not want us to get there either!

You are gravely mistaken if you do not recognize the reality of Satan and his demon followers ever present in our lives, our countries, our colleges, our schools, our neighborhoods, our societies—everywhere!

Watch out and think twice. Pray for guidance and for help. Most people cannot see evil spirits, but they are here.

Flee evil and choose good. Beware: *bad actions and bad people* **sometimes appear good.**

These evil beings are highly skilled at *making things seem good, when in reality, they are really bad.* **They are also experts at** *tricking people, families, and even nations.* (See Revelation 20:3)

Evil brilliantly seems innocent and harmless. That is the plan to undermine and destroy every one of us without us even recognizing what has actually happened. Frequently, people don't catch on until it is too late.

Take a good look at your life. Often evil works to get us to destroy ourselves and even those we love. **Make any necessary changes to get on the right paths.** It is critical. It's okay to ask for help. We all need help.

Jesus cast out evil spirits

(See Mark 1:24, 16:9; Luke 7:21; Matthew 4:24, 12:22)

When Jesus was on Earth, He cast out many evil spirits from people. In the Bible, there was a man who had multiple evil spirits (or devils) inside of him that caused many problems. The man was always, night and day, "crying, and cutting himself with stones." (Mark 5:5) Jesus asked him, "What is thy name? And he answered, saying, My name is Legion: for we are many." (Mark 5:9)

So, these many devils asked Jesus to not send them out of the country. "And all the devils besought him [Jesus], saying, Send us into the swine [pigs], that we may enter into them." (Mark 5:12 [Matthew 8:30-32 and Luke 32-33])

Jesus did as the devils requested. "And the unclean spirits went out, and entered into the swine: and the herd ran violently down a steep place into the sea, (they were about two thousand;) and were choked in the sea." (Mark 5:13) The man who was possessed with the devil and many evil spirits was now sitting with Jesus, clothed and back in his right mind. (See Mark 5:15 [For the whole story, see Mark 5:2-20]; see also Mark 16:9 and Luke 8:2 regarding Jesus casting out seven evil spirits from Mary Magdalene)

Evil is real. Be careful and wise.

Always remember that God and Jesus are much more powerful than evil. They are continuously ready to help us; we just have to ask.

$$\sim\sim\sim$$

What effect does the War in Heaven have on our daily life and long-term choices?

Satan and his army of demons expertly cloak their presence on Earth from everyday people. Their ultimate goal is to stay hidden and under the radar so no one believes they actually exist. People often consider them to be merely a joke. By concealing their existence, they are able to lurk about and influence negative choices, decisions, and occurrences. We must be ever cautious and vigilant, or we will inadvertently find ourselves on the wrong side.

It is important to note that most Bible translations **clearly tell of the War in Heaven and recount the story of Satan and his army of demons being banished from Heaven and sent to dwell on Earth.** Certain wording may be different (e.g., cast out vs. hurled down), but the overarching theme, story, and result remain the same.

(Examples: ASV—American Standard Version, CB—Catholic Bible, CSB—Christian Standard Bible, ESV—English Standard Version, KJV—King James Version, NCB New Catholic Bible, NIV—New International Version, NKJV—New King James Version. RSV—Revised Standard Version. See Revelation Chapter 12, in the New Testament)

Stay vigilant and always alert!

Blessings and Gifts
from Heaven

God gives us numerous wonderful gifts.
We often take many of them for granted.

God gave us **freedom** to choose whether we do **good or bad** things. This is extremely important so we can learn and grow. God gave us this freedom. When you think about it, it is pretty incredible.

Consider your five senses: they are God's gifts—like seeing, hearing, and having a brain so we can learn. Hands so we can touch and pick up items, even play the piano, clarinet, or guitar. Legs so we can run and jump and dance. Arms so we can give hugs and get **hugs.**

Positive feelings are a great blessing. We can be happy or joyous, or have fun and laugh, and especially feel love. Love is one of the best gifts of all.

Smiling is a gift. Each day is better when we smile, and smiles are contagious! When you give a smile, you often get a smile in return. Take a moment and think of more wonderful gifts we have been given, like the sunshine and snow.

Watch out for Satan's traps!

Now, feelings also come with a negative side. These negative feelings act as a warning to us. Many people ignore their feelings, but it is very important to acknowledge what you feel.

There is a special secret about feelings that everyone needs to know. The negative feelings hurt you the most and cause you endless problems when you bury them and keep them hidden inside your heart.

Dwelling in and on negative feelings is where the trouble begins. Satan and his crew will work diligently to keep you to focused on the bad stuff. When you allow yourself to be kept in the negative, it will change your life and who you become…and you hand Satan a win!

Think about someone you know to whom this has happened. Often, they are angry, bitter, or sour. Do not let that happen to you. Do not give Satan a victory.

Everybody has bad things happen at some point in their life. Do not let the negative things change who you were meant to be. Focus on the positive, whether you are 10 or 110, because

you are who *you choose* to be.

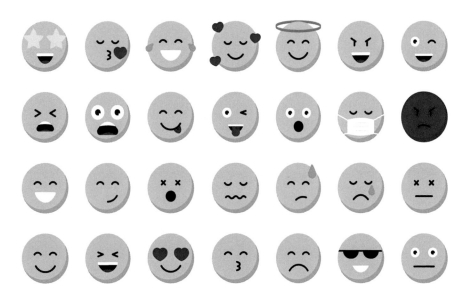

It is important to recognize *what* you are feeling!

It is much easier to deal with, handle, understand, and control your feelings when you actually know what they are. It makes all the difference in how you act and respond. Instead of your feelings being in charge of you, you learn to regulate and master them. This results in you having way more power and influence over your life and your destiny.

God really wants to hear from you and wants you to tell Him what you are feeling. Even though He already knows everything, God wants you to tell Him yourself.

The Best Parts Are Coming

When Jesus was about thirty years old, *He started His ministry.* *Jesus's ministry is one of the crucial purposes for which He was born.* We are getting to the best parts of all.

Jesus's cousin, John the Baptist, started his ministry long before Jesus began His. John preached about repentance and baptized many people, preparing them for Jesus. John said, "There cometh one mightier than I after me, the latchet of whose shoes I am not worthy to stoop down and unloose. I indeed have baptized you with water: **but** he shall baptize you with the Holy Ghost." (Mark 1:7-8; see Luke 3:16 and John 1:27)

Jesus Is Baptized.

"…John seeth Jesus coming unto him, and saith, *Behold the Lamb of God, which taketh away* the sins of the world." (John 1:29, emphasis mine)

John also said, "And I saw, and bare record that *this is the Son of God.*" (John 1:34, emphasis mine)

When Jesus was baptized by John the Baptist (see Matthew 3:16 and Luke 3:22), something incredible happened. "And straightway coming up out of the water, he saw the heavens opened, and the Spirit like a dove descending upon him: And there came a voice from heaven, saying, *Thou art my beloved Son, in whom I am well pleased."* (Mark 1:10-11, emphasis mine) A remarkable experience for all who were there. *No wonder so many people wanted to follow Jesus.*

Jesus said of John the Baptist, "For I say unto you, Among those that are born of woman there is not a greater prophet than John the Baptist." (Luke 7:28) John the Baptist told those who followed him that they should now follow Jesus.

Andrew had been following John. Andrew found his brother, Simon "Peter." Andrew told Peter that they found the Messiah, the Christ! Then Andrew brought Peter to see Jesus. (See John 1:40-41)

Peter was a fisherman, as were many others. One night after meeting Jesus, they had fished all night but caught nothing. Jesus told Peter to cast his nets again. Reluctantly, Peter did, and to his surprise, they caught so many fish that the ship began to sink. This was a miracle Peter needed to see, and it removed any doubts Peter had of Jesus being the Messiah.

"When Simon Peter saw it, he fell down at Jesus' knees, saying, Depart from me; for I am a sinful man, O Lord." (Luke 5:8)

"And Jesus said unto Simon [Peter], Fear not; from henceforth thou shalt catch men." (Luke 5:10 [see also Luke 4-10)

Many of Jesus's miracles were to show the disciples His divinity.

One by one, Jesus picked His twelve disciples/apostles (they are called both) to help Him to teach and help the people.

They were "Simon, (whom he also named Peter,) and Andrew his brother, James and John, Philip and Bartholomew, Matthew and Thomas, James the son of Alphaeus, and Simon called Zelotes, and Judas the brother of James, and Judas Iscariot, which also was the traitor." (Luke 6:14-16)

Forgiveness or Revenge?

Jesus taught the people and His disciples about forgiveness. It is important to understand that this kind of forgiveness was not part of Jewish law. Jewish law focused on what seemed to be justice and *getting even*. They called it "an eye for an eye, and a tooth for a tooth." (Matthew 5:38)

Jesus introduced a new teaching. This new kind of *forgiveness was a new concept.*

There are places in the Old Testament where **God forgave** His people, but the people themselves were not forgiving. Before Jesus promoted forgiveness, it was customary for people to seek revenge. For example, if you *accidentally* knocked someone's tooth out, then they could knock your tooth out to make things even..

Equally, if there was a horrible *accident* and someone's child was killed, then the child of the person who caused the accident could be killed to make things even. How was that fair to the second child or fair to that child's mother or siblings?

It was not, but that was the law for thousands of years before Jesus arrived. Wouldn't it be better to help console the family who lost their child, rather than cause another family an atrocious loss and grief? *Jesus conveyed these types of ideas and solutions over revenge and getting even.*

Jesus taught people about a higher law.

People forgiving each other is a higher law. This concept had never been promoted or considered in Jewish traditions or communities prior to Jesus's teachings.

Jesus taught everyone to choose to be good, to help others, and to forgive those who had wronged them in any way.

Who Is Perfect?

REALIZE HOW BLESSED YOU ARE

There is something that everyone needs to know and understand:

We need to be good, and we need to work on that every day. However, no matter how hard we try, *sometimes we will make mistakes*. We are going to mess up. *All* of us are going to make mistakes or sin. We *cannot* be perfect, even if we really want to be perfect. *We just cannot do it.*

Some people may *seem* like they are perfect or *think* they are perfect, *but they absolutely are not. Only Jesus is perfect.* "For all have sinned, and come short of the glory of God." (Romans 3:23) Jesus is the only one who has never sinned, and that is how He saves us.

God the Father is a God of Justice, and the demands of justice must be met. He is also a God of Mercy. So, a plan had to be created to fulfill both. Jesus fulfilled the demands for justice by *giving* His innocent, sinless life for our sins, making *mercy* possible for us. Mercy now could override justice, so we could be saved. Mercy is available for anyone who will follow Jesus and all His teachings and accept the mercy He provides. That will help us get to Heaven and live forever with our Father in Heaven and Jesus Christ.

This is how Jesus makes it possible for us to get the very best gift of all—forgiveness! Remember, Jesus paid the price for our sins so we can have mercy. Otherwise, those who don't follow Jesus will be facing justice for all they did in this life. Mercy is a much better choice, and the option is available to all. It took a lot of love for Jesus to do what He did for us.

Jesus Loves You.

When Jesus was on Earth, He taught everyone who would listen about our Father in Heaven and about choosing to be good and do good and going to Heaven. Ultimately, it is our choice. We all need to aim for Heaven and being with God and Jesus Christ forever!

Forgiveness is to be used when you sin or make a mistake. There is a great example in the New Testament where a woman had certainly done something bad. The crowd was going to stone her to death, which was the law at that time. "Stoning," as it is called, was a punishment often used where people threw so many rocks at the guilty person that they died. The woman was very afraid. The people had rocks in their hands, ready to throw. However, Jesus was there, and they looked to Him to see what He would say.

Jesus "said unto them, He that is without sin among you, let him first cast a stone at her." (John 8:7)

The people thought about what Jesus said. "And they which heard it, being convicted by their own conscience, went out one by one." (John 8:9) They each dropped their rocks and left. None of them was without sin, like us. Finally, not one person from the crowd was there. Only the guilty woman and Jesus remained.

Jesus told the woman, *"Go, and sin no more."* (John 8:11) He did not say, "Go do whatever you feel like doing." He said, *"Sin no more,"* which is an important part of forgiveness. To be forgiven, we need to actually be sorry for what we did wrong and work hard to not do that same wrong thing ever again.

"Then spake Jesus again unto them, saying, I am the light of the world: he that followeth me shall not walk in darkness, but shall have the light of life." (John 8:12)

In reality, what God just wants us to do is what most every good parent tells their kid when going onto the playground—"Always be nice, be kind, and play fair." Not too much to ask at all.

Jesus also taught about a new kind of love—a love where we forgive one another. This is a selfless love. It is easy to love people who love you back, like family and close friends. However, it is much harder to love people you do not know or even like. But we can do it.

Jesus taught us how, and He and Heavenly Father will help us. Once you learn to be forgiving, it actually becomes very easy. Much easier than you ever thought it could be, and the freedom feels wonderful!

CAUTION CAUTION CAUTION CAUTION

Forgiveness does not mean that you accept being treated badly! You should **never** allow anyone to be mean or bad to you or hurt you in any way. You are supposed to love yourself and take care of you.

If a relationship is not good or healthy, it is important that that relationship end. Forgiveness does not mean you have to have an ongoing relationship. It is okay to never see that person again, even if they are a relative. In fact, in some situations, it is better and healthier that you **never** have that person in your life.

Sometimes, we forgive to be free of the past or awful people and not let them hurt or control us or make us become bitter or sour. Forgiving *never* means condoning what happened. **Forgiveness = freedom and moving on to better times.**

CAUTION CAUTION CAUTION CAUTION

Repent

Repentance is necessary. We are **all** in need of repentance. Jesus said, "Except ye repent, ye shall all likewise perish." (Luke 13:3,5) If you ever talk to someone who has done bad things and then been forgiven, that means they *repented*—**they said they were sorry and tried to make up for their wrongs and not do them again**. That is called *repentance*. People who have *repented* will tell you how much better they feel about themselves and their life.

Repentance is always available.
Sometimes repentance is hard work. So, once you get yourself to a good spot, it is much easier to stay there. You do not want to have to achieve it again.

God will give you strength for every step of what you need:

"Be strong in the Lord, and in the power of his might. Put on the whole armor of God, that ye may be able to stand against the wiles of the devil.

"For we wrestle not against flesh and blood, but against principalities, against powers, against the rulers of the darkness of this world, against spiritual wickedness in high places.

"Wherefore, take unto you the whole armor of God..."
(Ephesians 6:10-13)

Learning to Love Yourself!

Everlasting life is a phenomenal principle.
Jesus made that possible for us.

We all need to forgive ourselves and accept the gift of
forgiveness that Jesus has *given* to us.

You also need to *learn to love yourself!* You are worth it.

It is easier to love yourself once you forgive yourself.

Learning to Love Yourself

Sadly, in today's world, many people loathe themselves or at best, dislike themselves immensely. That happens often when you rely on other people to give you your self-esteem or self-worth. Satan works overtime to make this happen. Truthfully, some people would be arrested if they treated their neighbor the way they treat themselves. You need to love *you* and be good to *you. Sometimes that takes hard work and prayer.*

We also need to learn to forgive ourselves. For some people, this is hard to do. They may be able to forgive others but cannot forgive themselves. This is when you need prayer and many conversations with God. He understands and will help. Remember, we have ***all*** sinned and made mistakes.

Forgiving yourself will help you in learning to love yourself.

Depending on your current and past situations, learning to love yourself may be the hardest path you will ever undertake. We have become way too critical and judgmental of ourselves. Part of that comes from valuing other people's opinions over our own or God's.

It is good to take an honest assessment of where you are. However, that does not mean you beat yourself up over everything. That is what Satan wants us to do—focus on the negative. You must and **need to** focus on the positive! Chances are, you have not killed anyone or weigh 1,200 pounds. Start there. **Make** yourself see some positives. **Let yourself have a sense of humor** along the way.

Seriously, make a list of positives and have some fun with it. You are worth the time and effort. As you recognize, encounter, or notice things you want to change, simply do it. Under **no** circumstances are you to beat yourself up about anything! **You cannot change the past.** You can only control **now**, and you do not want to waste one second on the negative. **Negativity steals lives** and precious moments.

To be clear, there are self-centered, spoiled brats around, as well. If you are one of those, **stop it immediately.** Many put on a facade of loving themselves, but deep down they don't even like themselves. **You too can change** and even become a **truly** nice person. It is horrible to feel like a phony and think that if people knew the real you they would not like you at all. Make the necessary changes to become authentic.

73

Wherever you are currently, following Jesus and focusing on the positive will help get you where you need to be. We will learn more about forgiveness and other helpful tool on our journey. Step by step, you can get to a fantastic place in your life.

Right now, you need to know four things:

1) ***God and Jesus love you.***

2) Focus only on the ***positive.***

3) ***Only Jesus Christ is perfect.***

4) ***You need to love you!***

Remember, only Jesus is perfect, and you need to love ***you***.

I need to love me, too!

Jesus also taught us to love one another—to love everybody, not just family and close friends. This was a newer kind of love, a higher love that He introduced to us and the world.

"Jesus said unto him, Thou shalt love the Lord thy God with all thy heart, and with all thy soul, and with all thy mind. This is the first and great commandment. And the second is like unto it, Thou shalt love thy neighbor as thyself." (Matthew 22:37-39) Thy neighbor means everyone. That is a lot of love.

Love makes the world a much better place.

As you become kinder to others and yourself, accept the forgiveness and love Jesus offers, and decide God and Jesus know way more than the people you have been letting control you, a miracle happens—you begin to feel better about you. Then you start to want everyone to feel good and happy too. You want to share the joy!

Receiving Answers from God

Jesus asked the disciples, "Whom say ye that I am? And Simon Peter answered and said, Thou art the Christ, the Son of the living God." Jesus said, "…Blessed art thou…for flesh and blood hath not revealed it unto thee, but my Father which is in heaven." (Matthew 16:15-17; Mark 8:29) Now, the disciples knew for certain who Jesus truly is, even though they did not yet understand everything.

Everyone wanted to be around Jesus—to hear Him, to touch Him, to be healed or blessed by Him. Jesus helped and loved many people.

Jesus wants us to help others, too. One of the best things we can do is to help people get to know Jesus. We can do lots of other things, as well. Sometimes, **just listening** is a tremendous help. **Listening** is a talent.

Listening to what God is trying to let you know is crucial! It takes practice, but you will learn—like Peter did.

Jesus Did Amazing Things and Performed Many Miracles

Jesus did *AMAZING* things.

"For God sent not his Son into the world to condemn the world; but that the world though him might be saved." (John 3:17)

Jesus performed many miracles. He made blind people see and the crippled able to walk. He even raised people from the dead.

Jesus walked on the water to join the disciples in the boat. The disciples were afraid when they saw Jesus walking on the water, until He said, "Be of good cheer: it is I; be not afraid." (Mark 6:49-50; John 6:19-20)

Jesus walked on the water and calmed the storms.

Jesus was asleep in the boat at night with the disciples when a bad storm came. The disciples were afraid and woke Jesus. "He arose and rebuked the wind, and said unto the sea, Peace, be still. And the wind ceased, and there was a great calm." (Mark 4:39)

The disciples "feared exceedingly, and said one to another, What manner of man is this, that even the winds and the sea obey him?" (Mark 4:41; Matthew 8:27)

The disciples were astonished by all the things Jesus could do. With every miracle they witnessed, their belief in Jesus and His purpose grew stronger.

Jesus did so many miraculous things because His discipled needed to be prepared for what was to come. They needed to be spiritually strong and grasp God's whole plan in order for it to succeed. Jesus also needed to strengthen and teach His followers.

Jesus said, "I am come that they might have life, and that they might have it more abundantly. I am the good shepherd: the good shepherd giveth his life for the sheep." (John 10:10-11)

Even though Jesus told the disciples repeatedly what was going to happen, they did not fully understand what was coming.

Jesus Taught Important Principles to Thousands

In the Sermon on the Mount, Jesus taught lessons like:

"Blessed are they that mourn: for they shall be comforted.
Blessed are the meek: for they shall inherit the earth.
Blessed are they which do hunger and thirst after righteousness: for they shall be filled.
Blessed are the merciful: for they shall obtain mercy.
Blessed are the pure in heart: for they shall see God.
Blessed are the peacemakers: for they shall be called the children of God." (Matthew 5:4-9)

"Blessed are ye, when men shall revile you, and persecute you, and shall say all manner of evil against you falsely, for my sake. Rejoice, and be exceedingly glad: for great is your reward in heaven." (Matthew 5:11-12)   For the entire sermon, see Matthew Chapter 5.

Jesus did many miracles.

Jesus and His disciples were at a wedding, and the wedding party ran out of wine. Mary, His mother, asked Jesus to help. Even though He was not ready to do public miracles, Jesus actually turned water into wine. (See John 2:3-11) It the very first public miracle Jesus ever performed.

Jesus fed over five thousand people with just five loaves of bread and two fish. After everyone had eaten until they were full, there were twelve baskets of food left. (See Matthew 14:17-21) He performed many astonishing miracles and helped countless people. Everyone was amazed by all the things Jesus could do, even His disciples.

Do you think it's a coincidence that there were twelve baskets of food left over and there were twelve disciples, and they would better understand the miracle that just happened?

"The blind receive their sight, and the lame walk, the lepers are cleansed, and the deaf hear, the dead are raised up, and the poor have the gospel preached to them." (Matthew 11:5; Matthew 12:22, 15:30-31, 21:14; Luke 7:22)

Jesus healed the blind.

The lame could walk.

Lepers were cleansed.

The deaf could hear.

The dead were raised.

Lazarus

Lazarus, Mary, and Martha were siblings and friends of Jesus. The sisters sent word to Jesus that Lazarus was sick, but Jesus did not come then. Jesus waited. He later said to His disciples, "Lazarus is dead. I am glad for your sakes that I was not there, to the intent ye may believe; nevertheless let us go unto him." (John 11:14-15)

They went to see Lazarus. By the time they arrived, Lazarus had been dead and in the grave (tomb) for four days. Mary and Martha were upset that Jesus had not come sooner and healed Lazarus.

"Jesus said unto her [Martha], I am the resurrection, and the life: he that believeth in me, though he were dead, yet shall he live." (John 11:25)

"And whosoever liveth and believeth in me shall never die." (John 11:26)

Jesus said, "Take ye away the stone. Martha, the sister of him that was dead, saith unto him, Lord, by this time he stinketh: for he hath been dead four days." (John 11:39)

"Jesus said unto her, Said I not unto thee, that, if thou wouldst believe, thou shouldest see the glory of God?" (John 11:40)

They removed the stone and *Jesus "cried with a loud voice, Lazarus come forth.* And he that was dead came forth." (John 11:43-44)

Can you imagine how incredible it must have been for those people seeing dead Lazarus alive again?

People not only came to see Jesus but also to see Lazarus, whom He had raised from the dead. (See John 12:9)

Faith
Brings Miracles

Faith brings miracles.

"And, behold, a woman, which was diseased with an issue of blood twelve years, came behind him [Jesus], and touched the hem of his garment." (Matthew 9:20) She was completely healed just by touching Jesus's garment.

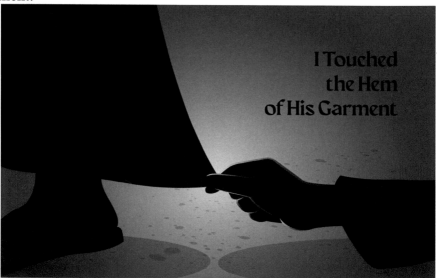

I Touched
the Hem
of His Garment

Many others sought Jesus "that they might only touch the hem of his garment and as many as touched were made perfectly whole." (Matthew 14:36)

Have you ever had a miracle?

Miracles really do happen!

To receive or be given a miracle, you have to *believe* in miracles! Jesus taught, "If ye have faith as a grain of mustard seed, ye shall say unto this mountain, Remove hence to yonder place; and it shall remove; and nothing shall be impossible unto you." (Matthew 17:20, emphasis mine)

A mustard seed is tiny—about the size of a grape seed or smaller. We can move mountains with the smallest bit of faith. What incredible power! We all need to increase our faith and believe.

Many individuals have experienced miracles; they are gifts from God. If we are not receiving miracles, we need to check our unbelief and **pray** for **more faith.** (See Matthew 13:58)

Jesus is very wise. Why do you think He taught the following? It is an important question.

"Whosoever shall smite [hit] thee on thy [your] right cheek, turn to him the other also.

"If any man sue thee [you] at the law, and take away thy coat, let him have thy cloak also.

"Whosoever shall compel thee to go a mile, go with him twain [two]." (See Matthew 5:39-41)

Back when Jesus was on Earth, the Romans ruled the Jewish area, and the Roman soldiers would hit the Jewish people and make them carry heavy loads for a mile. Whatever the soldiers chose to do, the Jewish people had to endure. Objecting only made things worse.

In each of these three statements, Jesus is teaching us to **not feel like a victim. Take charge of the situation.** We can see in each example how someone could go from being angry and upset or feeling victimized to knowing they had taken control as much as they could of what was transpiring.

This advice still applies to all of us today.

The people saw and experienced Jesus performing miracles, including raising the dead. They loved his kindness, his caring, and listening to His teachings. Everyone prepared for a feast. "When they heard that Jesus was coming to Jerusalem, [they] Took branches of palm trees, and went forth to meet him, and cried, Hosanna: Blessed is the King of Israel that cometh in the name of the Lord." (John 12:12-13)

Palm Sunday

As the people cheered, Jesus made a triumphant entrance into Jerusalem, riding on a donkey. They were excited to see Him. The people waved palm branches and laid the palm branches down in front of Him as a celebration of Jesus. This became known as **Palm Sunday**, the Sunday before Easter. Palm Sunday has been celebrated each and every year since.

Jesus said, "The hour is come, that the Son of man should be glorified." (John 12:23)

Jesus made the following abundantly clear: "Whosoever therefore shall confess me before men, him I will confess also before my Father which is in heaven. But whosoever shall deny me before men, him I will also deny before my Father which is in heaven." (Matthew 10:32-33)

Jesus said, "I seek not mine own will, but the will of the Father which hath sent me." (John 5:30) Jesus always does the will of our Father in Heaven. "I do nothing of myself, but as my Father hath taught me..." (John 8:28) "And he that sent me is with me: the Father hath not left me alone; for I do always those things that please him." (John 8:29) "I seek not my own glory." (John 8:50)

About three years into His ministry, *Jesus knew the two main reasons for His earthly ministry were soon to be revealed to the masses.*

Jesus knew He would soon be leaving and returning to His and our Father in Heaven. (See John 13:1)

Jesus had a last meal with His disciples, called the Last Supper. Jesus knew what was about to happen and that His disciple, Judas Iscariot, would betray Him. "And supper being ended, the devil having now put into the heart of Judas Iscariot, Simon's son, to betray Him." (John 13:2) Jesus said to Judas, "That thou doest, do quickly." (John 13:27) None of the other disciples knew what that meant.

Justice?
Or Mercy?

Judas left. Although Jesus knew what was about to happen, the remaining eleven disciples were unaware. Soon, Jesus and the eleven went to the Garden of Gethsemane. Jesus asked the disciples to keep watch while He prayed.

As Jesus prayed to God, He began taking upon Himself the sins of the world for *us* so we can be *forgiven* of all our sins and go to Heaven. It was extremely painful. "And being in an agony he prayed more earnestly: and his sweat was as it were great drops of blood falling down to the ground." (Luke 22:44) Despite the pain, Jesus prayed to the Father, "Thy will be done." (Matthew 26:42) Remember, Jesus always does the will of His Father and ours.

Thus began the *exchanging of justice* (an eye for an eye and a tooth for a tooth) *for mercy.* "For all have sinned, and come short of the glory of God." (Romans 3:23, emphasis mine)

Judas betrayed Jesus for thirty pieces of silver. Judas brought the Roman soldiers to where Jesus and the disciples were gathered. Judas walked up to Jesus and kissed His cheek so the soldiers would know which one was Jesus. "But Jesus said unto him, Judas, betrayest thou the Son of man with a kiss?" (Luke 22:48)

The Roman soldiers and some Jewish leaders came to arrest Jesus at the direction of jealous Jewish leaders. Some of the disciples tried to fight to protect Jesus. Peter even cut off the right ear of the high priest's servant. (John 18:10) Jesus healed the servant's ear and stopped the fighting. Jesus wanted peace. He went with the soldiers, even though He had done nothing wrong. He was taken to be put on trial.

Various Jewish leaders felt threatened by Jesus because He taught new ideas, like *people forgiving* and *loving everybody.* These Jewish leaders always wanted justice and ***never*** mercy. They were the ones who pushed for Jesus to be arrested so that they could get rid of Him.

The Jewish leaders who liked Jesus were not told about the trial, so they were not there to defend Him. The jealous Jewish leaders were using the Roman laws to have Jesus killed because the Jewish laws did not allow them to sentence Jesus to death. This was especially true since Jesus had done nothing wrong.

Many people gave false testimony against Jesus. Even with the lies and deceptions spoken in court, ***there was no evidence to warrant killing Jesus.*** Pontius Pilate, the Roman governor of that region, knew that Jesus was *innocent* and tried to set Him free. Ultimately, cowardice prevailed and Pontius Pilate gave into the shouts of the crowd, sentencing Jesus to be crucified—a horribly painful death. Pontius Pilate "took water, and washed his hands before the multitude, saying, I am innocent of the blood of this **just** person: see ye to it." (Matthew 27:24, emphasis mine)

Pontius Pilate's self-declaration of innocence did not make it so. He, too, was part of Jesus's false sentence. We all need to do what is right and stand up for others, even though it is sometimes hard.

Jesus was brutally beaten with a whip and made to carry His own cross. "With His stripes we are healed." (Isaiah 53:4-5)

Jesus suffered torment and excruciating pain. His hands and feet were nailed to the cross, and He was crucified. He died for all of us to pay the price for our sins.
In agony, Jesus willingly gave His life for us.

Upon Jesus's sacrificial death, mercy, instead of justice, became possible for every one of us. God and Jesus love us that much!

They placed Jesus's dead body in a tomb. It was the tomb of Joseph of Arimathaea, who was one of the Jewish leaders who would have defended Jesus had he known about the trial. The Jewish authorities made certain the huge stone in front of Jesus's tomb was sealed tight and well guarded. (See Matthew 27:62-66)

The Easter Miracle!

The Very Best Part Is Coming

"The angel of the Lord descended from heaven, ...and rolled back the stone from the door." (Matthew 28:2)

On the third day, Mary Magdalene went to the tomb, but the tomb was empty. Jesus was *gone*. Instead Mary found two angels there. "And seeth two angels in white sitting, the one at the head, and the other at the feet, where the body of Jesus had lain." (John 20:12) "Why seek ye the living among the dead? He is not here, but is risen." (Luke 24:5-6) Where was Jesus?

BEHOLD the Easter Miracle!

*Jesus was alive and He would **never die** again—*
He had been resurrected!

*Jesus came back to life and will **live forever**.*

Jesus stood outside of the tomb and told Mary, "Touch me not; for I am not yet ascended to my Father: but go to my brethren, and say unto them, I ascend unto my Father, and your Father; and to my God, and your God." (John 20:17)

Jesus said, "I lay down my life, that I might take it up again. No man taketh it from me, but I lay it down myself. I have power to lay it down, and I have power to take it again. This commandment have I received of my Father." (John 10:17-18)

"But we believe that through the *grace* of the Lord Jesus Christ we shall be saved." (Acts 15:11, emphasis mine)

Note:
Being raised from the dead (like Lazarus) means the person will die again. Being resurrected means you will ***never die*** *again*.

Remember when Jesus said, "Destroy this temple, and in three days I will raise it up." (John 2:19; Mark 15:29) Jesus was talking about the temple of His body and the resurrection, but no one understood it at that time. (John 2:21)

At various times Jesus plainly told the disciples what was going to happen and that He would rise on the third day, but they did not comprehend what He was telling them.

"For he [Jesus] taught his disciples, and said unto them, The Son of man is delivered unto the hands of men, and they shall kill him; and after that he is killed, he shall rise on the third day. But they [the disciples] understood not that saying." (Mark 9:31-32; see also Matthew 20:19; Mark 10:34; Luke 18:33, 24:7, and 24:46)
Once they saw resurrected Jesus, they understood!

The crucifixion of sinless Jesus Christ overcame sin and justice, making *mercy available for us!*

We are saved by grace through Jesus Christ.

"For by grace are ye saved through faith; and that not of yourselves: it is the gift of God." (Ephesians 2:8)

Two women came to the tomb. *"And the angel answered and said unto the women, Fear not ye: for I know that ye seek Jesus, which was crucified. He is not here: for he is risen, as he said..."* (Matthew 28:5-6)

CHRIST IS RISEN

The Resurrection of Jesus Christ overcame death and brings eternal life. Our Heavenly Father and Jesus Christ want *each* of us to make it to Heaven and live with Them forever.

The choice is ours. **It is up to us.** *They will help us* make it if we try, ask, and repent when needed, trying to "sin no more." (See page 68)

YOUR DAILY CHOICES REALLY MATTER!

~CHOOSE WISELY~

After His resurrection, Jesus appeared in many places. "At evening…
when the doors were shut where the disciples were assembled for fear of
the Jews, came Jesus and stood in the midst, and saith unto them, Peace
be unto you." (John 20:19)

Jesus showed them His nail-scarred hands and His side, where a Roman
soldier stabbed Him with his sword while Jesus was on the Cross. "Then
were the disciples glad, when they saw the Lord." (John 20:20)

Jesus said to the disciples, "As my Father hath sent me, even so send I .you." (John 20:21)

"And when he had said this, he breathed on them, and saith unto them, **Receive ye the Holy Ghost."** (John 20:22)

Thomas was not with them when the other disciples saw Jesus. Thomas was skeptical and doubted what the disciples said about Jesus. Thomas said, "Except I shall see in his hands the print of the nails, and put my finger into the print of the nails, and thrust my hand into his side, I will not believe" (John 20:25).

After eight days, Thomas and the disciples gathered again. Jesus came and said to Thomas, "Reach hither thy finger and behold my hands; and reach hither thy hand, and thrust it into my side: and be not faithless, but believing." (John 20:27)

"Thomas answered and said unto him, My Lord and my God." (John 20:28)

Jesus said, "Thomas, because thou hast seen me, thou hast believed: *blessed are they that have not seen, and yet have believed."* (John 20:29)

Thomas is often referred to as "Doubting Thomas." Thomas did not have faith. Do not doubt, have faith!

"Go ye therefore, and teach all nations, baptizing them in the name of the Father, and of the Son, and of the Holy Ghost: Teaching them to observe all things whatsoever I have commanded you: and, lo, I am with you alway[s], even unto the end of the world. Amen." (Matthew 28:19-20)

"In my Father's house are many mansions ... I go to prepare a place for you." (John 14:2)

"I will come again ... that where I am, there ye may be also." (John 14:3) ("may" be—**up to us!**)

103

The disciples needed to be brave and resolute because Jesus would soon leave Earth and return to our Father in Heaven. They needed to continue His ministry. Jesus promised the disciples that the Holy Ghost, the comforter, would come to help them.

Jesus also told them:

"Peace I leave with you, my peace I give unto you... Let not your heart be troubled, neither let it be afraid.

"Ye have heard how I said unto you, I go away, and come again unto you. If ye loved me, ye would rejoice, because I said, I go unto the Father: for my Father is greater than I." (John 14:27, 28)

~~~~~

Jesus prayed for His followers.:

"I pray for them: I pray not for the world, but for them which thou hast given me." (John 17:9, emphasis mine)

"I pray **not** that thou shouldest take them out of the world, but that thou **shouldest keep them from the evil."** (John 17:15, emphasis mine)

"Neither pray I for these alone, but for them also which shall believe on me through their word." (John 17:20, emphasis mine)

The Ascension

It was a magnificent and miraculous time.

Jesus spoke to His disciples one last time, giving them instructions for the ministry. And then "while they beheld, he was taken up; and a cloud received him out of their sight. And while they looked steadfastly toward heaven as he went up, behold, two men stood by them in white apparel;

which also said, Ye men of Galilee, why stand ye gazing up into heaven? This same Jesus, which is taken up from you into heaven, shall so come in like manner as ye have seen him go into heaven." (Acts 1:9-11)

They were referring to **the Second Coming of Jesus Christ**.

The disciples watched as Jesus ascended into Heaven, and they began to better understand all of the things Jesus taught them.

Jesus is the Christ.

He is the long-awaited Messiah.

Jesus lives and will come back to Earth at His Second Coming!

The disciples were with Jesus for His earthly ministry. Now, they had to carry the ministry forward with Jesus gone. Jesus trusted them to do that.

They did an incredible job, many even giving their lives.

~~~

Recall that in the story of Moses, the lamb's blood on the front door frames saved the firstborn Israelites from death. That event was a foreshadowing of *the blood of Jesus Christ, the Lamb of God,* **saving us** *from our sins and eternal death and exchanging* **justice for mercy**.

We all need mercy! Jesus died so we could have it.

Jesus Christ,
the Lamb of God
and our Savior

So, WHY is Jesus?

1) Jesus taught us to love everyone, not just our family and close friends.

2) Jesus taught us that we should forgive. "And forgive us our debts, as we forgive our debtors." (Matthew 6:12)

3) Jesus *gave* us the *gift of forgiveness* so that we can be forgiven. You cannot buy it or earn it—it is a gift. We just have to accept it.

4) Starting in the Garden of Gethsemane, Jesus began taking upon Himself all the sins of everyone who will follow Him. "And being in an agony … his sweat was as it were great drops of blood falling down to the ground." (Luke 22:44)

5) Jesus was Crucified and died for **our** sins and **for us** so that we could be saved.

6) Jesus overcame death and was Resurrected, making resurrection possible for all of us. We just need to follow Him and do what is right. If and when we mess up, we repent.

7) Jesus fulfilled the demands for justice by *giving* His innocent, sinless life for our sins, making *mercy* possible for us. Mercy now overrides justice so that we can be saved.

8) Jesus made it possible for us to choose to go to Heaven and be with Him and our Father in Heaven. **Our choice.**

9) *"Through the grace of the Lord Jesus Christ, we shall be saved."* (Acts 15:11, emphasis mine)

10) Jesus made it possible for us to live forever!

~~~And more...~~~

"Jesus said unto her, I am the resurrection, and the life: he that believeth in me, though he were dead, yet shall he live: **And whosoever liveth and believeth in me shall never die.**" (John 11:25-26)

"For God so loved the world, that he gave his only begotten Son, that whosoever believeth in him, should not perish, but have everlasting life." (John 3:16)

Of the people you love the most, who would you let innocently suffer and die the way Jesus did? You do not have to answer that question. It just points out *how much God loves you*. He allowed Jesus to *suffer and die for us* because *He loves us that much*. Jesus was *willing* to suffer and die **for us** because *He loves us that much, too*.

That's a lot of love!

Jesus told us, "In the world ye shall have tribulation: but
be of good cheer; I have overcome the world."
(John 16:33)

Developing Your
Superpowers

There are five **superpowers** we all need.

Two of these **superpowers** are regarding feelings.

The first *superpower* is *recognizing* what you are feeling—name the feeling so you know what it is (e.g., mad, sad, glad, frustrated, lonely, happy, etc).

Write it down. ***Writing things down always helps you learn and remember them.*** Learning and remembering are important steps in developing this *superpower.*

The second *superpower* is *talking* about what you are feeling with another person. Make a list of your feelings and who you can talk to about them: a parent, grandparent, family member, teacher, doctor, Sunday school teacher, friend, neighbor, or your co-worker. Choose someone you can trust.

Don't forget to add God, our Heavenly Father, to your list. The great thing is, *God is always available, and you can talk to Him about anything and everything.*

Not yet ready to live with your feelings? Grab a stuffed animal and start talking: even talking to a stuffed animal will help—regardless of your age.

Why does mastering these two *superpowers* matter? When you are unable to *recognize your feelings,* you are lost. When you are unable to *talk about your feelings,* you are out of control. When these two negative powers unite, Satan has the upper hand.

Picture a very tightly wound ball of yarn. Hold it in your hand and squeeze. It's tough and hard, right? Imagine being hit in the face with that tightly wound yarn ball—it's solid and it hurts! Can you cut through that ball with a pair of scissors? No! No matter how many times and ways you try, that ball of yarn is too tough, and it can be used to ***hurt you.*** Repeatedly.

Now, grab the loose end of that yarn ball. Let it start to unwind. It becomes just a long, thin, soft piece of string. Imagine being hit in the face with a piece of that yarn—it's flimsy and you barely even notice. Can you cut through that yarn? Yes! You can cut it into as many pieces as you want, and those bits and pieces of yarn can't be used to cause you harm.

When your feelings stay buried inside, Satan will orchestrate ways to keep hitting you with that ball of yarn. He will rearrange those tightly wound strings to trip you up, cause you torment and grief, and then he will add even *more* string around that ball with each mistake you make. **Don't let that happen!**

Satan is clever, but you can outsmart him. *Recognizing your feelings* is like holding that ball of yarn. *Talking about your feelings* is like unraveling that ball.

Use your *superpowers* and ask those you trust, and God, for help. Heaven is on your side and will help more than you realize. When you unravel your feelings, it helps neutralize Satan's power against you!

~~~

Understanding what you are feeling and talking about those feelings with someone you trust will save you much sorrow. It may seem scary at first, but it will help you tremendously.

Remember, **when your feelings get buried inside of you,** the devil has more power and ability to use them against you, and buried emotions **can ruin your life!** Employ these two *superpowers*, and Satan will not be able to cause you as much trouble as he would like.

Recognizing and talking about your feelings can result in many *positive life changes. God and Jesus will help you! They always want the best for you.*

Woohoo!
Use your superpowers, and you will be winning.

Feelings and **Prayer**

God really wants to hear from *you* and wants you to tell Him what and how you are feeling. Even though God already knows everything, He really wants to it hear from you.

Afraid to pray or think you don't know how to pray? Think of it as a conversation; just talk to God. As you put time into prayer, you will grow closer to Him each day. In turn, you will learn how to identify your feelings and will actually get to know yourself better.

It is much easier to handle, understand, and control your feelings when you actually know what they are and identify them. It makes all the difference in how you act and respond. Instead of your feelings being in charge of you, you learn to regulate and master them. You end up having way more power and influence over your life *and* your destiny.

Choosing to pray on a regular basis or choosing to not pray at all will absolutely change who you become! This is one of the most important decisions you will ever make in your life. Choose the right path. You and your family will be thankful that you did.

God loves to hear from us anytime and all the time.

God and Jesus are always there, *waiting to hear from us.*

Flourishing with Forgiveness

Learning to *forgive* the way Jesus taught is the next *superpower* we can unlock. When you don't forgive, you **relive** the awful moment(s) over and over again. Nobody wants that. It makes it hard to get away from what happened and move forward. Instead of being miserable about something that happened in the past, when you *forgive*, you move on to happiness. Don't stay stuck in misery, anger, sadness, or seeking revenge.

Sometimes, it is very hard to forgive until you have experienced the **freedom** it offers you. There are times you have to work and **pray hard** for that first forgiving experience, but **the freedom feels wonderful**. It makes your life much happier when you get the *forgiving superpower*.

Now, not everybody gets this **superpower** right away. *You may need to let God rev up your heart to get this one. It takes some practice.* Keep praying for help to forgive. It will happen!

What happens when someone faces something that is not humanly possible to forgive? It truly is unforgivable.

Unfortunately, there are some **very bad, even horrific, and horrendous** things that happen. If you find there is something that you cannot forgive, *give it to God*.

You can explain it in prayer, or write Him a note about the situation and shred it, bury it, or burn it. Writing helps. Whatever works for you.

God knows and will understand. Let Him handle whatever you cannot forgive so you are not chained to it, tormented by it, carrying it around, and reliving it every day of your whole life. Giving it to God brings you **freedom** so you can move on to fun and happiness.

Anger destroys.

There was a staunch Christian who was devastated when a child in her family had been physically and emotionally abused in a horrible way. The woman was so shattered by what happened she could no longer pray the way she had for years. So, when she prayed, she said, "I don't know what to say, but I don't want to totally lose contact." That is all she prayed twice a day for six months.

The woman was very angry with God but questioned who was she to be mad at God. This kept her from being honest with God and herself.

Finally, one day, she broke down and told God how angry she was, and she could not understand how He allowed this to happen. She ended up spending hours on the floor in prayer, pouring out her heart with a flood of tears and expressing her wrath that she had been holding back.

To her surprise, what she learned was that not only was God brokenhearted *and* angry over what had happened but that He loved the little girl even more than she did. The woman had never considered any of that.

This Christian also got a lesson in *free will*— how important it is and that one day *all things will be made right*. God wants us to be honest with Him and ourselves, even when we are angry—respectfully, of course, but honest. Give the horrible things in your life to God. Let Him handle it all so you can move on to joy. The devil wants us in misery.

Do not let the devil steal your joy!

Remember, being good and doing good is *way* better than making wrong or bad choices.

To get to Heaven, we *all* need *forgiveness*. However, we also need to *work at being good and doing good* and rely every day on the forgiveness that Jesus made possible for us *for the stuff we cannot fix or undo*. There is a lot of that.

We all need to learn to forgive and love others. Forgiveness comes through desire and prayer. Sometimes, it takes lots of prayer.

Consider an important point some of you may be asking yourself: "Why should I be good if I can just get forgiveness?" Well, the answer is very simple: You get blessings from being good. The fact is that God really wants to bless us and has millions of blessings just waiting to be given. Ultimately, *we* stop ourselves from receiving countless blessings by making wrong choices. So, it is much better to be good and reap all the blessings we can get. Also, if we have more blessings, we are in a better position to help others.

Make right choices and let those blessings shower down on you every day.

Is Forgiveness Real?

There are places throughout the New Testament where Jesus and His disciples cast out devils and evil spirits. The Bible states that "...Mary Magdalene, out of whom he [Jesus] had cast seven devils." (Mark 16:9) In addition, in Luke it says, "And certain women, which had been healed of evil spirits and infirmities, Mary called Magdalene, out of whom went seven devils." (Luke 8:2) So, it is evident that Mary Magdalene used to have seven devils within her that had to be cast out. Mary Magdalene became one of Jesus's most devout followers.

However, the New Testament also says, "Now when Jesus was *risen* early the first day of the week, he appeared *first* to Mary Magdalene, out of whom he had cast seven devils." (Mark 16:9, emphasis mine) Ponder that for a moment. The *very first* person Jesus saw and talked to after leaving His tomb was Mary Magdalene, even before His disciples. **If you ever doubt forgiveness being real, recall these events. Jesus is extremely serious about forgiveness.** Do not hesitate to ask for help.

What Now?

Blessings await. God wants to bless us more than we could ever imagine. It is **totally up to us** to choose to do what we need to do to receive those glorious and wonderful blessings.

We **all** face huge problems, trials, and obstacles at times, but God will *always* **help us** if we turn to Him.

Heavenly Father and Jesus Christ can and will change things for the better.

We just need to do our part, ask, and let them.

Remember, you are worth the effort!

126

We just learned a summary of the story of Jesus. Now that you have the basics, you can journey deeper.

You can learn much more by reading the New Testament in the Bible. A good place to start is the book of John, the fourth book of the New Testament. After you read John, try reading Matthew, Mark, and Luke. Then Acts and Romans. Read all the New Testament and find out for yourself which is your favorite book.

Jesus prepared the way.
We just need to follow His path and His teachings.

It is good to read the Bible and pray every day. Doing so gets you tuned in. It's kind of like the old radios that had to be tuned to the right frequency or you could not hear anything but static. The more we are tuned into Heaven, the more we learn, and the more help we receive. Listening is the key.

Unleashing Your Superpowers

Superpowers We All Want and Need:

Honesty
Recognizing what you are feeling
Talking about what you feel
Forgiving
Prayer

Prayer is so important that we are adding it to our **superpowers** list. It will help you considerably with all your **superpowers**. Praying is the most important **superpower** you have, although, ironically, the other four will help you with your prayer life and prayer response. Having these **superpowers** will give you a much happier, successful, and better life.

Praying should be the foundation of everything we do! It is the support for all you need to happen and all you want to accomplish. Having this **superpower** can actually make you a partner with God. You can experience more Heavenly power than you ever imagined! You will be thankful you did.

Praying is important and easy. It is how you get to know God and yourself better. Some people think it is hard and don't pray because they think they aren't good enough. However, God wants to hear from you no matter what your circumstances. (And remember, *only Jesus is perfect.*) Do not let feeling inadequate or thinking prayer is hard keep you from praying; it is simple. Jesus taught us how to pray. (See Matthew 6:9 and Luke 11:2)

5 Easy Steps to Prayer ...and wonderful life changes that are possible.

Get on your knees, and—

1) *Just call on God by one of His names, respectfully:*
"Dear God" or "Father in Heaven" or "Heavenly Father."

2) *Thank Him for what is good in your life or what has happened that day.*

3) *Tell Him what you need or want, asking for His help.*
(Yes, God already knows everything, but He wants to hear it from us. This is how you get to know Him and yourself better—by deciding and speaking about what you *really* need or want.)
It also reminds you that when the blessings come, God did that for *you. He really is listening.*

4) *Pause and listen* before you close your prayer.
If a thought comes to your mind, pay attention to it. God may be telling you something.

5) *Pray "Thy will be done" as Jesus did, and end your prayer in the Name of Jesus Christ. Amen.*

(More miracles come from praying the phrase "Thy will be done" than any other. It may be hard, but it is important. God knows what is right and best for us, and that is not always what we think we need/want.
Remember, to get miracles, you must believe in miracles.)

That's it. That is all you need to do.

Praying morning and night is a great basic habit. As you get to know God better, you will find that you may want to pray more than twice a day, and that is fantastic. (See also Matthew 6:9-13)

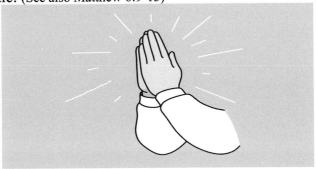

131

Exploring Another Superpower

Honesty

You may have noticed that we skipped *honesty*. Even though *honesty* is the first *superpower* on our list of five, we are addressing it last. It is so important to be *honest*, especially with yourself. It helps with all your other *superpowers* and tremendously *increases your walk and communication with God and Jesus.*

So, why are we doing it last, you ask? Simply put, people are **extremely protective and defensive about their lies,** especially the ones they tell themselves. Learning what we have to this point, hopefully, will **lessen those protective barriers and destructive defenses.** Knowing and understanding that God and Jesus Christ offer and give help will also increase your odds of success. Heaven is rooting for you and wants the best possible outcome for your life and your eternity.

Lots of people lie. Some become so jaded by it, they hardly notice any more that they are even lying. It almost becomes like breathing—it happens without thought. Many others refer to their lies as "little white lies," trying to make them seem harmless.

However, who lies hurt the most is *you*, the teller. Eventually, they completely *destroy your* **trust** in everybody. (If you are not trustworthy, who can you trust?) Not to mention all the friendships and relationships you lose along the way. People do not like to be lied to, and even though you may get away with some lies, you eventually *will* get caught. *Lying definitely changes who you are and who you were meant to be!*

There is another problem with lying. People sometimes lie to themselves even if they don't have a habit of lying to others. This is dangerous territory. They are just avoiding reality, which causes a different set of problems. ("My wife would never cheat on me." "I have the best boyfriend ever.")

Whereas, we hope these statements are true, sometimes untrue statements allow very bad behavior and cause people to accept horrible treatment.

Often, liars lie to themselves or others frequently.

Before they know it, their life is a complete mess, and they've lost the relationships, job, opportunities, and hope that they were telling the lies to try to keep. Lying ends up hurting *you*. Just don't do it. ***Live in honesty*** and peace. You will feel way better about yourself and you will have a much happier and better life.

The old adage that you either *are* or you *are not* pregnant holds true for honesty. There is no middle ground. You either *are* or you *are not* honest! Do not lie. **Choosing honesty works wonders** in your life and self-esteem. It also greatly increases your connection with God, Jesus, and Heaven. As well, it is a Commandment—not a suggestion. Refer to #9 of the Ten Commandments. **Honesty is that important.**

Reality Alert!

Having Trouble Forgiving?

Changing Your Understanding of Forgiveness

Let's change your understanding of forgiveness. Forgiveness is not for the person who wronged you; *forgiveness is your release* from having been wronged. It's not for them—it's for *you*.

Chances are, the person who wronged you will never think of what they did to you again. They likely won't remember it, or don't even care. How, then, does reliving those terrible moments over and over again and again help you? Why dwell?

Picture yourself on a hike. In front of you is the tallest mountain you've ever climbed. You have a big backpack filled with large rocks. The zipper on your backpack is stuck. You have to carry all those rocks for the entire hike. The load becomes heavier and heavier as you go. How far will you make it up the mountain?

Now, picture yourself on this same hike, going up the tallest mountain, with your rock-filled backpack. Only this time, *you* get your zipper unstuck. After every fifty steps, you toss a rock. The load gets lighter and lighter as you go. **You are getting the hang of forgiving and letting go**

133

of the garbage that has been weighing you down and stealing your happiness. How far will you make it up the mountain?

The Unforgivable!

Unfortunately, some acts are so heinous, it feels utterly impossible to forgive. So, what do you do in this case when something is humanly impossible to forgive? *You give it to God!* When human forgiveness is out of your reach, open your heart and lay it all out for God. You can still find freedom and be released from these wrongs. Let Him take your pain. He can handle it, and He knows how to set things right for you—*you just have to let Him.*

Once more, picture yourself on this hike, going up the mountain, with your rock-filled backpack. No matter what you do, the zipper is stuck. That load is weighing you down and becoming heavier as you go. The stuff inside is just so horrible you **desperately want to be free** from it, but you just can't let it go! **You ask God for His help.** God unzips His backpack and puts your whole backpack inside His. Now, *God's got it all* so you can be free from the awful burden. How far will you make it up the mountain?

Brooding on all the sins visited upon you, holding grudges, and living in the past only hurts *you.* Forgiveness provides a freedom like no other. Do you want to be stuck or do you want to you free?

Unzip that backpack and toss those rocks or give them to God so you can make it up the mountain!

Gaining a
Great Life!

The Start and Stop Path to Success

Change can be one of our biggest challenges. Some people are able to make all the changes they want at one time. However, for most people, going step by step brings long-lasting and permanent results.

Try ***The Start and Stop Path to Success.***
First, **Start** doing **one** thing that you need to do.

Praying is a great first choice. If you are not yet bringing God and heavenly help into your daily life, start here. If you already have a good prayer life, work on something else good.

Second, **stop** doing **one** thing that you should not be doing.

Continue to start one good thing and stop one bad thing. Following this path, you will achieve complete success before you know it!

Remember, writing things down helps. (A spiral notebook works great. It is also inspiring to look back and see how far you have come.)

If you mess up, **start** again and **stop** beating yourself up. Only Jesus is perfect. (Although, don't use that as an excuse.) You want to progress forward to receive all the blessings that are waiting for you.

Understanding Spiritual Experiences

If you have never had a spiritual experience, you may find it hard to understand the phenomenal impact it can have. Most people go from "thinking" or "hoping" God is real to "knowing" He exists.

In the New Testament, Paul tells us, "The natural man receiveth not the things of the Spirit of God: for they are foolishness unto him: neither can he know them, because they are spiritually discerned." (1 Corinthians 2:14)

You must have a willingness and a desire to believe in order to experience the things of God. You also have to be teachable as a child is teachable.

People who share their personal spiritual experiences often stop sharing because they are met with unbelief, ridicule, and even attacks. They quickly understand the warning given in Matthew, "Give not that which is holy unto the dogs, neither cast ye your pearl before swine, lest they trample them under their feet, and turn again and rend you." (Matthew 7:6)

This does not mean that spiritual experiences and miracles don't happen; they happen frequently. It only means that believers are cautious about the people with whom they share their experiences. That is exactly what Satan wants to happen—unbelief and fear can both be crippling and lead to a self-created imprisonment.

Do not let skepticism or unbelief keep you from getting or seeing miracles and having spiritual experiences. Also, do not let fear, disguised as wisdom or discernment, keep you from sharing what you have experienced when you should.

Be strong and courageous for Christ!

To be clear, our Father in Heaven is real, Jesus Christ is real, Heaven is real, miracles are real, spiritual experiences are real. Satan is real, demons and evil spirits are real, and Hell is real.

Hope and pray you learn these truths before it is too late!

~~~~~~~~

Words Matter

Words Either Heal or Destroy!

Making Critical Choices

Your words and your actions are conduits for inviting people into your life, heart and home. The same is true for good or evil. Daily, even hourly, **your words and your actions invoke either the presence of God or the presence of the devil into your life!**

People unknowingly summon Satan simply by continuing their bad habits. The most prolific example is using curse words. Satan is thrilled to receive these little invites, especially because folks don't realize that their bad habits allow evil to flourish. It's Satan's bread and butter. Without much, or any, thought, you just do the same bad thing over and over and unintentionally fuel Satan's evil fires. You inadvertently become trapped right where Satan wants you—like a frog in a pot, unaware the water's slowly starting to boil.

On the other hand, God wants us to *consciously choose Him* by inviting good into our lives. He wants us to *live life purposefully.* When creating habits, make certain they are good ones. Think before you speak. This intentional practice is so important that Jesus and His disciples warned us about the words we choose:

"Not that which goeth into the mouth defileth a man, but that which cometh out of the mouth, this defileth a man." (Matthew 15:11)

"Do not ye yet understand, that whatsoever entereth in at the mouth goeth into the belly, and is cast out into the draught? But those things which proceed out of the mouth come forth from the heart, and they defile a man." (Matthew 15: 17 and 18, emphasis mine)

"Let no corrupt communication proceed out of your mouth, but that which is good to the use of edifying, that it may minister grace unto the hearers." (Ephesians 4:29)

"With their tongues, they have used deceit; the poison of asps is under their lips: whose mouth is full of cursing and bitterness." (Romans 3:14)

"But now ye also put off all these, anger, wrath, malice, blasphemy, filthy communication out of your mouth." (Colossians 3:8)

"Out of the same mouth proceedeth blessing and cursing. My brethren, these things ought not so to be." (James 3:10)

Choose who you are!
Choose God and Jesus every day, in every way.

Now What?

Many people *know about* our Father in Heaven and Jesus Christ. However, *knowing* our Father in Heaven and Jesus Christ is completely different. Having a *relationship with Them is amazing.* It can and will change your life in ways you never imagined.

The easiest way to cultivate a relationship with God and Jesus is:

1) *Be honest with yourself.* Stop making excuses for yourself or others in your life. Take an honest look to see if there are changes you need or want to make. As mentioned, write things down. It helps.

2) Pray to our Father in Heaven honestly and completely in the Name of Jesus Christ. Pour out your heart to Him and bare all your soul to Him. Yes, He already knows everything, but He wants you to *trust* Him enough to tell Him *everything.* He also wants to know that you actually *recognize who you are* and that you are willing to *admit who you are to Him and to yourself.* This is when real change can happen.

3) *Thank* our Father in Heaven for any and all the good in your life. No matter how bad things are, there is always something to be thankful for. (Things can always be worse.) Do not ignore the negative things in your life, but try focusing on the positive. Whether you **focus** on the negative or the positive, *that* is what will multiply in your life. *It is much better to invite in good and positive things than anything negative.*

Henry Ford said, "Whether you think you can or whether you think you can't, you're right." He was spot on! Think about that statement and let it soak in for a while.

4) *Ask for help.* God will help you. Never hesitate to ask for help. You will be astounded at what can happen.

Remember these two rules:

A) God only helps with things that are **good** and **positive** for us. (Sometimes, we want what is **not** good for us.)

B) God will **never** take away another person's **free will** in order to give us what we want. He does **not make** people do things; **we choose**.

Until is the key.

Work **until** you have a relationship with our Father in Heaven and Jesus Christ. Never give up. It **will** happen.

Being a Christian is not something reserved for Sunday mornings. It is **who you are** all of the time.

$$\sim\!\sim\!\sim$$

Recall the War in Heaven and remember that Satan and his evil demons are on Earth.

Right now, the war is at hand!

Everyone must pick a side. If you do not choose good, evil will choose you. Your inaction will increase Satan's ability to cause you more harm.

Peter warned us, "Be sober, be vigilant; because **your adversary the devil, as a roaring lion, walketh about, seeking whom he may devour."** (1 Peter 5:8)

Devouring people's souls and destroying their lives is what Satan does daily!

There are some good television pastors and ministers to watch. However, it's a good idea to *find a church to attend*. You may even be surprised how many people help you and how many people *you* help.

Our Father in Heaven and Jesus Christ will help you get to where you need to be.

Remember, you are working to love yourself and to get you to a good spot. Keep going *until* that happens. Your life and your happiness matter that much.

"Choose you this day whom ye will serve; …but as for me and my house, we will serve the LORD."
(Joshua 24:15)

The Beginning

of *what you choose* to make of you.

Bonus
Features

The chains of sin are broken with the freedom of *forgiveness* Jesus provides for us.

"If God be for us, who can be against us?" (Romans 8:31)

God and Jesus are always there for us. God the Father, His Son Jesus Christ, and the Holy Ghost help us have a better life and to get to Heaven. We are the ones who withdraw or push Them away!

~ Heaven Awaits ~

Don't Be Afraid of the Bible—some excerpts

You may find it interesting that after Abraham came his son, Isaac, then Isaac's son, Jacob, and the twelve tribes of Israel. God changed Jacob's name to Israel. The twelve tribes are from Jacob's twelve sons.

Old Testament

"Be still, and know that I am God." (Psalms 46:10)

"The Lord is on my side; I will not fear: what can man do unto me?" (Psalm 118:6)

"Be of good courage, and he shall strengthen your heart, all ye that hope in the Lord." (Psalm 31:24)

"Trust in the Lord with all thine heart; and lean not unto thine own understanding. In all thy ways acknowledge him, and he shall direct thy paths." (Proverbs 3:5-6)

"Unto thee, O Lord, do I lift up my soul." (Psalm 25:1)

"In God have I put my trust: I will not be afraid what man can do unto me." (Psalm 56:11)

"In my distress I cried unto the Lord, and he heard me." (Psalm 120:1)

New Testament

"If we say we have fellowship with him, and walk in darkness, we lie, and do not the truth: But if we walk in the light, as he is in the light, we have fellowship one with another, and *the blood of Jesus Christ his Son cleanseth us from all sin.*" (1 John 1:6-7, emphasis mine)

"For where your treasure is, there will your heart be also." (Matthew 6:21)

"If ye love me, keep my commandments." (John 14:15)

"Let not your heart be troubled, neither let it be afraid." (John 14:27)

"With God all things are possible." (Matthew 19:26)

"Be not afraid, only believe." (Mark 5:36)

And this is life eternal, that they might know thee the only true God, and Jesus Christ, whom thou hast sent." (John 17:3)

"I can do all things through Christ which strengtheneth me." (Philippians 4:13)

"Jesus saith unto him, I am the way, the truth, and the life: no man cometh unto the Father, but by me." (John 14:6)

"Grace be unto you, and peace, from God our Father and the Lord Jesus Christ." (Colossians 1:2)

Start *your* treasure hunt.

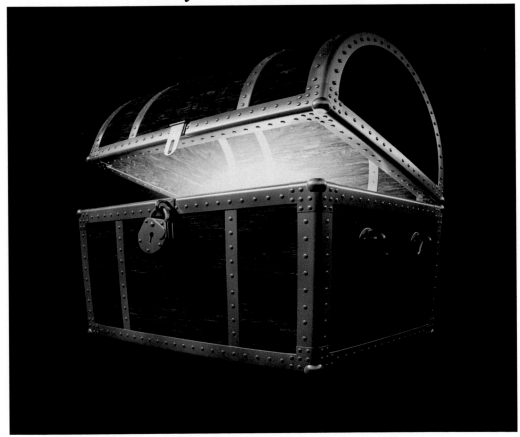

How many gems can *you* find in the Bible?

Jesus loves little children. They are innocent, honest, and pure.

Truth be told, we are all still kids inside.

We can work on being innocent and pure by accepting the forgiveness Jesus provides for us and following His teachings.

"Except ye…become as little children, ye shall not enter into the kingdom of heaven." (Matthew 18:3)

We can achieve honesty by making some changes, including being honest with ourselves.

Be willing to learn and change, like little children do.

Be very careful how you treat children!

Jesus said, "But whoso shall offend one of these little ones which believe in me, it were better for him that a millstone were hanged about his neck, and that he were drowned in the depth of the sea." (Matthew 18:6; see also Mark 9:42 and Luke 17:2)

Children who have had bad things done *to* them are victims and are *not* guilty, even if they have been made to feel guilty. They have *no* need of repentance for what has been *done to* them.

Many people work to make changes on the outside, but making changes on the inside is much more beneficial and lasting.

"Pleasant words are as an honeycomb, sweet to the soul, and health to the bones." (Proverbs 16:24)

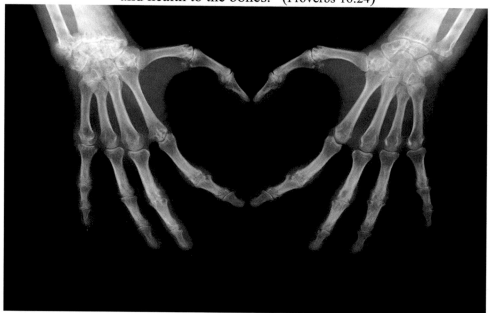

Work on having a heart of gold.

The Treasured Body
Your Body Is a Gift from God

The Old Testament says, "And God said, let **us** make man in **our image.**" (Genesis 1:26, emphasis mine) Our Father in Heaven was talking to Jesus. They worked together to create our body.

We often take our body for granted. However, when you really think about all the parts and how everything works, it is absolutely amazing.

Remember when we talked about loving yourself? You need to love your body, as well. Your body is the temple that houses your soul.

Cherish your body as the temple of your soul.

~~~

Satan's Sly Tricks Continue

Attacking Your Self-worth!

In today's world, people are very critical of their bodies. Many of the advertisements and social media posts often make people look superficially perfect when they are absolutely not. It is better to not compare yourself to others, but if you are going to compare, **do not** turn to media. That is **not** real. Look around your local grocery store, gas station, or shopping mall. Consider only real people, not fabrications.

Way too much focus is put on physical appearance, taking focus away from the more important spiritual part of ourselves. Want to take a guess who is responsible for all of us being so body conscious and body shaming? *Yes, you got it!* Satan himself. He influences many avenues of life in negative ways. What a sly way to attack people's self-esteem and undermine their self-confidence.

Once you understand what is happening, you become aware of much phoniness and superficial aspirations. Look good as you. Never try to be somebody else. Once you get to *know you*, you will find that *you are pretty spectacular.*

Always remember, our Father in Heaven and Jesus Christ love you!

Some Interesting Stuff for You to Explore on Your Own

- What happened when Jesus wanted to wash Peter's feet? (Read John 13:6-9)
- What happened when Peter tried to walk on the water to Jesus? (Read Matthew 14:28-32)
- What happened when the centurion (Roman soldier) asked Jesus to heal his servant? (Read Matthew 8:5-13 and Luke 7:1-10)
- What happened to Judas Iscariot? (Read Matthew 27:1-10)
- What happened when Mary was pregnant with baby Jesus and went to see her cousin, Elisabeth, who was pregnant with John the Baptist? (Read Luke 1:41-42)
- What did Herod's stepdaughter ask for after she completed her dance? (Read Mark 6:25)
- Jesus is known as the Good Shepherd. What did Jesus mean by "Feed my sheep?" (John 21:17)

***Challenge: After you have read the New Testament many times, how many places can you find in the Old Testament that are actually referring to Jesus Christ?

***Clue: Lots

Example: "Surely he hath born our griefs, and carried our sorrows ... he was wounded for our transgressions [that means sins], he was bruised for our iniquities: the chastisement of our peace was upon him; and

with his stripes we are healed." (Isaiah 53:4-5)

WHO IS JESUS?

We know that:

Jesus is the only begotten Son of God.

Jesus always follows God's directions and always does God's Will.

Jesus is the long-awaited Messiah.

Jesus is the Christ.

Jesus is the Savior of the world.

Jesus is our own personal Savior.

Jesus is the Alpha and Omega.

Jesus is pure love.

Jesus is forgiveness.

Jesus is eternal.

Jesus is our brother and our friend.

WHY IS JESUS? (Part 2)

Jesus *gave* His perfect, sinless life to replace justice so *we* can be **forgiven** through *mercy*.

Jesus taught us how to **love** Completely.

Jesus taught us how to **care** and to **give.**

Jesus taught the importance of good choices.

Jesus taught us to repent when we need to.

Jesus taught us how to truly forgive**.**

Jesus taught us to trust our Father in Heaven.

Jesus proved that **we are worth something.**

Jesus died so we could **go to Heaven.**

Jesus is Our Savior and Our Redeemer.

Most of all, Jesus **is** because we needed to be **saved.** —from ourselves and from Satan's evil.

Jesus makes our **life better every day** and helps us through the hard times.

Jesus provides us with a **choice between eternal happiness or regret.**
You choose.

Jesus makes it possible for us to have eternal life and live with Him and our Father in Heaven forever!

157

Paul taught us that "faith is the substance of things hoped for, the evidence of things not seen." (Hebrews 11:1)

Be a courageous Christian and stand up for Jesus.

It is the best decision you will ever make!

FAITH AND

COURAGE

go hand in hand.

You can have one or the other, but having them together makes each one stronger.

Courage means

*be scared
and do it
anyway*

Remember, it is okay to ask for help.

We always should!

It is good to help others when we can, too.

SAMPLE CHAPTER OF THE NEW TESTAMENT/BIBLE
(Not everybody owns a Bible)

John Chapter 3 (emphasis mine)

1 There was a man of the Pharisees, named Nicodemus, a ruler of the
Jews:
2 The same came to Jesus by night, and said unto him, Rabbi, we know
that thou art a teacher come from God: for no man can do these miracles
that thou doest, except God be with him.
3 Jesus answered and said unto him, Verily, verily, I say unto thee, Except
a man be born again, he cannot see the kingdom of God.
4 Nicodemus saith unto him, How can a man be born when he is old? can
he enter the second time into his mother's womb, and be born?
5 Jesus answered, Verily, verily, I say unto thee, Except a man be born of
water and of the Spirit, he cannot enter into the kingdom of God.
6 That which is born of the flesh is flesh; and that which is born of the
Spirit is spirit.
7 Marvel not that I said unto thee, Ye must be born again.
8 The wind bloweth where it listeth, and thou hearest the sound thereof,
but canst not tell whence it cometh, and whither it goeth: so is every one
that is born of the Spirit.
9 Nicodemus answered and said unto him, How can these things be?
10 Jesus answered and said unto him, Art thou a master of Israel, and
knowest not these things?
11 Verily, verily, I say unto thee, We speak that we do know, and testify
that we have seen; and ye receive not our witness.
12 If I have told you earthly things, and ye believe not, how shall ye
believe, if I tell you of heavenly things?
13 And no man hath ascended up to heaven, but he that came down from
heaven, *even* the Son of man which is in heaven.
14 And as Moses lifted up the serpent in the wilderness, even so must the
Son of man be lifted up:
15 That whosoever believeth in him should not perish, but have eternal
life.
16 For God so loved the world, that he gave his only begotten Son, that
whosoever believeth in him should not perish, but have everlasting life.
17 For God sent not his Son into the world to condemn the world; but that
the world through him might be saved.

18 He that believeth on him is not condemned: but he that believeth not is condemned already, because he hath not believed in the name of the only begotten Son of God.

19 And this is the condemnation, that light is come into the world, and men loved darkness rather than light, because their deeds were evil.

20 For every one that doeth evil hateth the light, neither cometh to the light, lest his deeds should be reproved.

21 But he that doeth truth cometh to the light, that his deeds may be made manifest, that they are wrought in God.

22 After these things came Jesus and his disciples into the land of Judaea; and there he tarried with them, and baptized.

23 And John also was baptizing in Aenon near to Salim, because there was much water there: and they came, and were baptized.

24 For John was not yet cast into prison.

25 Then there arose a question between some of John's disciples and the Jews about purifying.

26 And they came unto John, and said unto him, Rabbi, he that was with thee beyond Jordan, to whom thou barest witness, behold, the same baptizeth, and all men come to him.

27 John answered and said, A man can receive nothing, except it be given him from heaven.

28 Ye yourselves bear me witness, that I said, I am not the Christ, but that I am sent before him.

29 He that hath the bride is the bridegroom: but the friend of the bridegroom, which standeth and heareth him, rejoiceth greatly because of the bridegroom's voice: this my joy therefore is fulfilled.

30 He must increase, but I must decrease.

31 He that cometh from above is above all: he that is of the earth is earthly, and speaketh of the earth: he that cometh from heaven is above all.

32 And what he hath seen and heard, that he testifieth; and no man receiveth his testimony.

33 He that hath received his testimony hath set to his seal that God is true.

34 For he whom God hath sent speaketh the words of God: for God giveth not the Spirit by measure unto him.

35 The Father loveth the Son, and hath given all things into his hand.

36 He that believeth on the Son hath everlasting life: and he that believeth not the Son shall not see life; but the wrath of God abideth on him.

Congratulations, you just read a whole chapter of the Bible!